MEXICO CITY

MEXICO CITY

BY ROBERT PAYNE

PHOTOGRAPHS BY DICK DAVIS

HARCOURT, BRACE AND WORLD INC., NEW YORK

The quotations from the book *The Futile Life of Pito Pérez*,
by José Rubén Romero, translated by William O. Cord, © 1966 by
William O. Cord, published by Prentice-Hall, Inc., Englewood
Cliffs, N.J., originally published in Spanish under the title *La Vida
Inútil de Pito Pérez*, © 1964 by Carlos Romero Cuellar,
are reprinted by permission; those from *Cortés* by Francisco
López de Gómara, translated and edited by Lesley Byrd Simpson,
published by the University of California Press, Berkeley,
Calif., 1964, are reprinted by permission.

CONTENTS

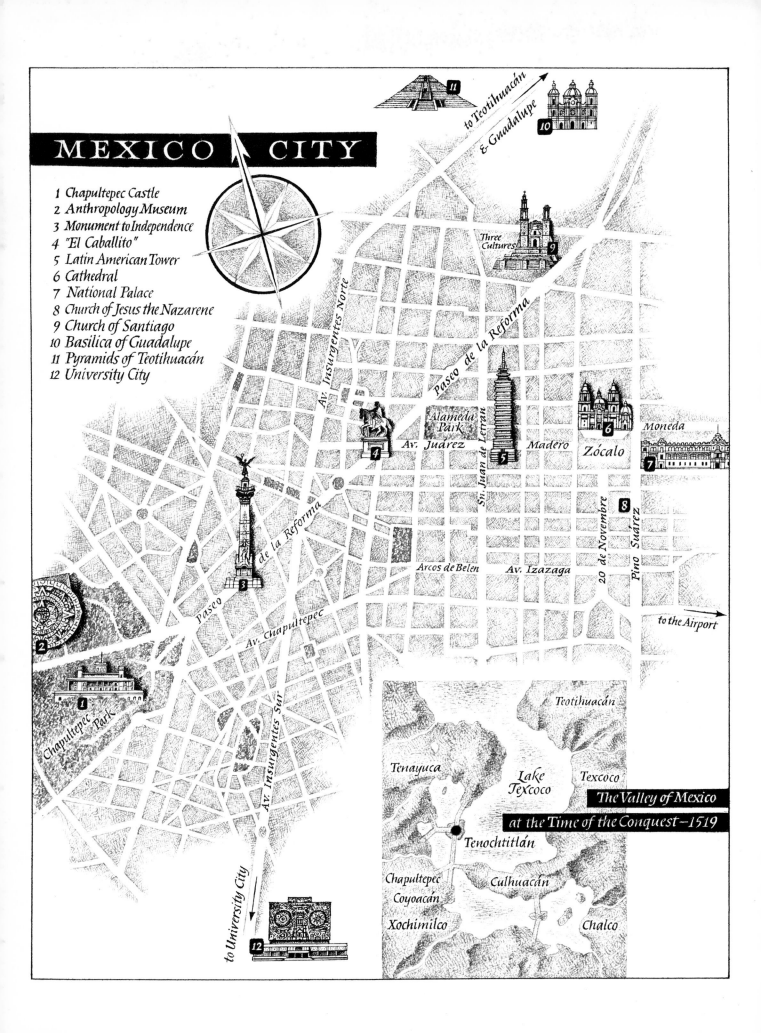

MEXICO CITY

1 Chapultepec Castle
2 Anthropology Museum
3 Monument to Independence
4 "El Caballito"
5 Latin American Tower
6 Cathedral
7 National Palace
8 Church of Jesus the Nazarene
9 Church of Santiago
10 Basilica of Guadalupe
11 Pyramids of Teotihuacán
12 University City

to Teotihuacán & Guadalupe

Three Cultures

Paseo de la Reforma

Alameda Park

Av. Juárez

Sn. Juan de Letran

Madero

Zócalo

Moneda

Av. Insurgentes Norte

Paseo de la Reforma

Av. Chapultepec

Arcos de Belen

Av. Izazaga

20 de Novembre

Pino Suárez

to the Airport

Chapultepec Park

Av. Insurgentes Sur

to University City

The Valley of Mexico
at the Time of the Conquest – 1519

Teotihuacán

Tenayuca

Lake Texcoco

Texcoco

Tenochtitlán

Chapultepec
Coyoacán

Culhuacán

Xochimilco

Chalco

MEXICO CITY

TENOCHTITLÁN

"We were amazed, and we said that it was like the enchanted things related in the book of Amadis because of the huge towers, temples, and buildings arising from the lake, and all of masonry. Some of the soldiers even asked whether the things we saw were not a dream. You must not wonder that I write of these things in this way, for it beggared all description, since we were seeing things which had never been heard of or seen before, nor even dreamed about."

So wrote the conquistador Bernal Díaz del Castillo about the day when he first set eyes on Tenochtitlán in the freshness of an early morning, remembering in old age his first glimpse of the enchanted city. Suddenly, beyond the mountain passes, he entered fairyland, and as he wrote he still felt a quickening of the blood and a thundering in his ears. He was writing when he was very old indeed, and half a century had passed since he had marched on Tenochtitlán as a young soldier, but it was all so fresh and vivid that he could have stretched out his hand and touched the vanished city of his dreams.

He was not alone in the belief that he had seen something so strange and wonderful that nothing like it had ever existed, or was ever likely to exist again. Hernán Cortés, writing to the Emperor Charles V, called it quite simply "the most beautiful city in the world," and so it was. There was a radiance about it, a shining splendor. It shone fiercely in the light of majestic blue skies, snow-white mountains, a calm blue lake. There was about this city, built on an island in the lake, an astonishing air of unreality, because it was too perfect, too beautiful, too richly decorated. Not Venice, nor Paris, nor Isfahan, nor any of the rose-red cities of India had such sumptuous elegance and soaring grace. As the early morning mist rose over the lake, the city seemed to shimmer and flash with all the colors of the rainbow. The green forests came down to the lakeside, the canoes were rushing about like so many brilliantly colored water beetles, the smoke rose from the temples, and there was that subdued quivering sound which comes when thousands upon thousands of people are going about their business. It was as though at a single moment of time an architect of genius had given himself the problem of building a perfect city and succeeded beyond all expectation.

To Bernal Díaz del Castillo and all the other conquistadors who entered the city peacefully on that clear November morning in 1519, the city came as a revelation, a sudden shock on exposed nerves. No one had so much as hinted to them that such perfection was possible. They had come up from the humid coastal plains, where there were only reed huts, and on their way they had passed through large and important cities like Cholula with its myriad temples, but Cholula was essentially provincial; they did not hold their breaths when they entered it. There was nothing in the least provincial about Tenochtitlán, the capital of a great empire. Power streamed from it; it flaunted its magnificence. Like Peking, like Athens, it commanded respect by its very beauty.

Mostly they were men from the harsh and arid plains of Estremadura, and very young. They were the sons of magistrates, lawyers, soldiers, merchants, and they knew Madrid and the great cities of Castile, and some had been to Venice. They knew what cities were like, but nothing in their experience had prepared them for a city that floated on the water like a white ship. In the book of Amadis cities spring into existence in the twinkling of an eye. Tenochtitlán looked so fresh that it might have been built the previous day.

Of course it had not happened like that. Innumerable architects had been at work over many years; priests and necromancers were consulted; and the Emperor, wearing a headdress of brilliant bluish-green feathers and sitting on a golden throne, had studied the plans and commanded what buildings should be renovated, or changed, or abandoned altogether, for he alone was the repository of the ancient traditions of his people. Always there was that sureness of hand, the certain knowledge of what must be done, the vision of the whole city unfolding before their eyes. There are color films showing a rose expanding from bud to full flower in a single minute, petal by petal uncurling and achieving a perfect harmony, so that at every moment the unfolding of the flower is wholly beautiful. The city of Tenochtitlán resembled a many-colored flower on the surface of a lake, and we can watch it unfolding.

Originally there was only a small white rocky island in a marshy lake. To this island in A.D. 1325 there came a tribe of hunters and farmers, who called themselves Aztecs, from Aztlán, a place far away in the northwest. They had entered the

The Colossi of Tula, columns that
once supported a thatch roof
at the base of a pyramid

Valley of Mexico two hundred years before, without ever settling down, sometimes taking service under local kings, sometimes foraging for themselves—a despised people, poor and unscrupulous. There was a legend among them that they would found a great empire when they came to a place where they saw a white willow, a white frog, a white fish, and an eagle poised on a cactus with a serpent in his talons. All these things were found when they came to the white island, and accordingly they set out to build a great city and a great empire.

They lived in reed huts on the island, worshiped the sun-god Huitzilopochtli, and sold fish, ducks, and water snakes to the neighboring towns, where no one suspected the newcomers planned to conquer them.

In this way, very slowly, there rose first the village, then the town, then the vast city of Tenochtitlán, which means "the place of the rock and the cactus." The first chieftain assumed the name of Tenochti. In his lifetime the island began to spread over the lake, for mud and silt dredged from the lake bottom were packed solidly around the rock, and in addition there was an ingenious system of man-made islands formed by cutting a system of parallel canals through the marshland and raising up beds of reeds and rotting vegetation between them. These islands, called *chinampas*, were then covered with topsoil and anchored at their corners with willows. Whenever the chieftain felt the need to widen the boundaries of the town, the man-made islands were transformed into dry land and new *chinampas* were built beyond them. The rich volcanic silt gave them several crop plantings every year. From this early period came the earthen pyramid built in honor of Huitzilopochtli in the very center of the island, on the site where they had seen the eagle with the serpent in his talons. Later they would build larger and more ornate temples of polished stone.

During the reign of Tenochti the lake dwellers began to invade the surrounding territory. The island was set near the western shores of a bay guarded at the north by Tenayuca and in the south by Culhuacán. They were both powerful cities, and Culhuacán was especially important, because many vassal towns belonged to it, and for many years the Aztecs had been slaves in the Culhuacán kingdom. That they should have succeeded in conquering their masters only whetted their appetite for more conquests, and in 1383, ten years after the death of Tenochti, they advanced deeper into enemy territory and conquered Cuernavaca. Then year after year there were more conquests, and one after another the tribes surrendered to

The great Olmec head of La Venta

the lords of Tenochtitlán. In the reign of Itzcoatlin, the fourth Tenochcan chieftain, the extent of Aztec rule had become so vast that it could already be called an empire. Tribute poured in from the distant cities, and the officers of the Aztec colonial office marched unarmed among the conquered tribes, secure in the knowledge that no one would dare to harm them.

Itzcoatlin, which means "Black Stone Snake," was the real founder of Aztec power. A thoroughly despotic ruler, he ordered the burning of the ancient chronicles of his people and set his scribes to writing a more heroic history. By his orders two great temples were erected in the sacred plaza, the inevitable one to Huitzilopochtli and the other to Coatlícue, the mother of the gods, whose face was two serpent heads and whose body was writhing serpents. She had been the supreme goddess ruling over the people of Culhuacán. The Emperor's mother had been a beautiful slave girl from Culhuacán, and the temple appears to have been built to honor the friendship between the two cities.

Under the Emperor Ahuítzotl, who reigned from 1486 to 1503, the city of Tenochtitlán assumed the form it would have when the Spaniards entered it—a vast metropolis surrounding a central plaza, with a population of about three hundred thousand people. Since Culhuacán and the goddess Coatlícue were no longer in favor, the original pyramidal temples were reworked and enlarged and rededicated to Huitzilopochtli and Tlaloc, the god of rain and fertility. The power of Ahuítzotl reached to the Pacific, and with his immense wealth, with trains of tribute bearers arriving daily at the capital, he was able to ensure that these temples would be more majestic than any others. These temples asserted the power of the Aztec gods, and by a necessary implication the power of the Aztec state.

The double temple to the sun and the rain rose from a base three hundred and thirty feet long, with two wide stairways leading to the summit; the private houses of the gods, built of wood, two stories high, and covered with gold leaf and vivid paint, stood on the upper platform. The doors were curtained with bright hummingbird feathers. The roof of Tlaloc's house was decorated with giant sea shells, for he was the god of the waters. The roof of Huitzilopochtli's was decorated with butterflies, symbols of the sun and fire. Above these houses rose roof combs, and these, too, were brilliantly painted. The double temple rose like a white cloud with bands of rainbow colors, dazzling in its beauty against the dark-blue Mexican sky.

Right
The Pyramid of the Sun, Teotihuacán

Next two pages
The "Avenue of the Dead," Teotihuacán

The double temple was a complex and astonishingly sophisticated work of art, all the proportions brilliantly calculated. The stepped pyramid with the two private houses of the gods was merely the basic element. Beyond this, with deliberate design, the Aztec architects went on to add the essential ornamentation: the balustrades of the stairways, which were decorated with feathered serpents seeming to plunge headlong to the ground, for their heads rested at the bottom of the pyramid. At the summit, too, there were statues of standard-bearers wearing imperial crowns of bluish-green feathers. On the stairway there stood an image of the sun, with symbols indicating the calendar devised to enable astronomers to determine the eclipses, for the Aztecs were obsessed with the passage of time and determined to penetrate its secrets. Time stood sentinel over the temple, for he was a god to be worshiped and placated like all the others.

The double temple dominated a vast plaza of polished stone, so smooth and shining that it resembled a mirror, reflecting the passing clouds and the starlight. Smaller temples stood within the enclosure. There was a new temple to Coatlícue, who had been deposed from her high estate but was still worshiped, and to Quetzalcóatl, whose temple took the form of a round tower and was entered through a portal carved in the shape of a wide-open serpent mouth. Altogether there were about seventy religious buildings in Tenochtitlán and most of them were to be found within the enclosure. There were treasure houses, arsenals, a monastic school, a musical academy, a ball court, and there was also a temple to all the foreign gods, known and unknown. In the complex arrangement of temples the great plaza at Tenochtitlán somewhat resembled the crowded summit of the Acropolis in Athens, where the huge statues of Athena and Poseidon on the pediment of the Parthenon presided over the smaller temples of the lesser gods.

Since the Emperors were always high priests, their palaces overlooked the temple enclosure. In the time of Moctezuma, Ahuítzotl's cousin and successor, three immense royal palaces were arranged along three sides of the square. On the ground floors, in vast colonnaded halls, were the quarters of the royal magistrates, the royal treasure houses, and the workshops where craftsmen and goldsmiths prepared the many ornaments needed by the sovereign; here, too, were to be found the royal menageries filled with rare tropical birds, jaguars, pumas, tigers, lynxes, and wolves, together with eagles and every known bird of prey. Swans and egrets swam in vast indoor pools. Serpents, from huge boa constrictors to harmless

Children climbing the Pyramid
of the Moon, Teotihuacán

water snakes, lay in cages or in earthenware jars. There were gardens filled with tropical trees, flowers, and medicinal plants, and there were more flower gardens on the palace roofs. No vegetables or fruit were grown in the royal gardens, for it was felt that the gardens must be for the pure enjoyment of the Emperor and must not serve any utilitarian purpose.

On the upper floors of the palaces were the private apartments of the Emperor, vast colonnaded halls inlaid with marble like a chessboard, with walls of marble and jasper, porphyry and basalt, and with roof beams of sweet-smelling cedar and cypress. Some rooms were painted with mythological scenes, others were carpeted with skins or worked feathers or embroidered cotton quilts, for there was no wool. In these rooms lived the innumerable women and servants of the Emperor, the princes of the tribes who came every year to pay tribute, and the hostages they left behind them. Here the Emperor received his guests, who even if they were great noblemen approached the throne on their knees, dressed in simple cotton robes to demonstrate their humility, saying over and over again: "Lord, my lord, O great lord."

The Emperor lived in great state, and his whims were the law of the land. But usually he had no need to express his power by giving way to his whims. He lived quietly, hidden from the world, ruling in secret. On the rare occasions when he entered the city, the people averted their faces from him or prostrated themselves. If he was walking, servants would run ahead of him and lay carpets at his feet.

For the Emperor there was reserved all that was strange and beautiful. If some hitherto unknown animal was discovered anywhere in the empire, it was immediately brought to him; a new flower or a new fruit became by its very newness the property of the Emperor; and he collected dwarfs, hunchbacks, and monsters, because they were strange and inexplicable. Wherever he gazed there were gardens and white soaring temples, pools and fountains, the glint of softly waving feather curtains and the brightness of hammered gold.

But it was in the market place that Tenochtitlán showed its brightest colors. Every city had its market place, but Tenochtitlán, being the capital, had the largest, the richest, and the most famous. Cortés wrote that sixty thousand people could be seen bartering in the square, which was twice as large as the square at Salamanca. Everything was done in an orderly manner; every trade had a street of its own; ten judges sitting under awnings high above the market place, saw to it that there

was no theft and settled quarrels promptly. The police patrolled the rows of shops, but they were rarely needed, for the people behaved with good sense and reason, quietly enjoying themselves.

There were streets for the goldsmiths and silversmiths, and for the merchants of slaves and caged beasts, of skins and hides, of ducks and pheasants and hummingbirds, of deer and rabbits and moles and the little edible dogs whose meat was sweet but whose skin was as tough as an elephant hide. There were barbershops, apothecaries, and herb vendors. Doctors examined their patients and prescribed ointments, salves, and infusions, and performed complicated operations on broken bones. The knowledge of herbal medicine was far advanced and more than twelve hundred varieties of medicinal herbs were made known to Dr. Francisco Hernández, the physician of King Philip II. There were restaurants and bathhouses. There were shops where brilliantly striped and patterned blankets were sold. There were vegetable shops, piled high with onions, leek, garlic, and gold thistles, and fruit shops, where the plums were especially prized for their sweetness. Honey and beeswax, corn syrup and sugar cane, the sweet juices of the maguey plant, and many colored confections of sugar and corn flour. Fish, fresh and salt, raw and cooked, was sold in abundance, for the people of Tenochtitlán were lake dwellers and their fishing fleets patrolled the lake. Fish came from the Atlantic in huge salt vats or still alive in tubs filled with salt water.

The Indians adored the market place, for it was their meeting place, the place where news, gossip, and rumor flourished. They were a gregarious people, and they enjoyed the noise and the tumult, the hours spent in cautious bargaining. Money took the form of gold dust, copper bells, cocoa beans. The gold dust filled the hollows of goose quills, and the exact amount of gold in a quill could be easily measured. Generally, however, they traded by barter, exchanging pottery for food, or blankets for jewelry, for nearly everyone wore some distinctive jewels or feathers, which were accounted to be as beautiful as jewels. A boy would walk along the street wearing a necklace formed of eight rows of pearls, and no one would think anything of it.

The Spaniards were particularly impressed by the excellence of the craftsmen. Francisco López de Gómara, the secretary of Cortés, paid special tribute to their goldsmiths and the workers in feathers. He wrote: "The most beautiful things in the market are the gold and featherwork, in which they make replicas of everything

in every color. The Indians are such masters of the craft that they will make a butter-fly, an animal, a tree, a rose, flowers, herbs, and rocks, all done with feathers, and with such fidelity that they seem alive or natural. So absorbed are they in placing, removing, and adjusting the feathers, scrutinizing them from one side or the other, in the sun, in the shade, or in the half-light, that sometimes they will not eat all day long. In a word, they will not let the work out of their hands until it is absolutely perfect. Few nations have such patience, especially the short-tempered ones like ourselves.

"The craft of the highest rank and greatest skill is that of the silversmiths, who bring to the market cast pieces of fine workmanship, set with precious stones: an octagonal plate, half of gold, half of silver, not soldered together, but joined in the casting; a small kettle, cast with its handle, as is done here in the casting of bells, but separately; a fish with silver scales and another of gold, regardless of how many scales it may have. They can cast a parrot that moves its tongue, head and wings; a monkey that moves its feet and head, and holds a distaff in its hands, so naturally that it seems to be spinning, or an apple that it appears to be eating. . . . They also make lacquerware; they set and carve emeralds, turquoises, and other stones, and bore pearls. . . ."

There was almost nothing they could not do. They could carve great blocks of basalt and porphyry, using no tools, for all that was necessary was immense patience and strings soaked with wet sand: the quartz in the sand would gradually cut through the huge blocks. They could carry vast blocks of stone over long distances on rollers, and they could build tunnels and aqueducts, like the great aqueduct that brought fresh water from Chapultepec to Tenochtitlán. The featherwork and the gold have vanished; only a few small feather tapestries remain, and most of the gold was melted down, but not before Albrecht Dürer saw it. "I marveled over the subtle genius of these men in strange countries," he said, after seeing the great gold plates, chased and engraved in rich designs, which Cortés sent to Charles V. "They were much more beautiful to behold than anything spoken of in fairy tales." This was the same joyful cry uttered by Bernal Díaz del Castillo. These artificers worked in strangeness and beauty, and nothing like these works of art had ever appeared in Europe.

The Aztecs were, in fact, far more civilized than the Spaniards. In everything we mean by "civilization"—in the arts and crafts, in the forms of government and

An Indian and her wares

administration, in the color and contentment of the people's lives, in the far-reaching organization of trade, and in the splendor of their architecture—they were superior to the Spaniards. Above all, they gave their people a way of life that was wholly satisfying, rich in poetry and song, with continual ceremonies and fiestas to illuminate the pageant of their days.

Above them stood the proud and lonely Emperor Moctezuma, who represented in his person all that was best in his race. When the Spaniards entered Mexico, he was forty years old, with dark glowing eyes and aristocratic features, his long black hair growing over his ears, with no more than a hint of beard. He was of a lighter color than most of the Indians, and he moved gracefully, like a dancer. Moctezuma means "the solemn and angry one," but he was rarely angry, and his solemnity derived perhaps from the years he had spent training for the priesthood. He changed his clothes four times a day, and gave his cast-off clothes to his servants and soldiers as a mark of his favor; he bathed twice a day; and he ate alone, served by four hundred page boys, while music was played for him by musicians hidden behind a screen of hummingbird feathers. No one ever counted the number of his wives and concubines or the number of his palaces, for he had palaces all over his empire. But what people chiefly remembered about him was a certain asceticism, a joyous disinterest in the panoply surrounding him, and his devotion to the gods. He enjoyed the choral dances in the courtyards of his palace, attended the ball games, took part in military maneuvers, and led his soldiers into battle, but there was always a reserve about him. Affable and well-mannered, calm and usually very self-assured, he concealed himself behind a screen of quietness. He took pleasure in walking quietly, for fear that his footsteps might resound like thunder.

Such a man at such a time might have possessed all the qualities necessary to lead his people against a foreign invasion. He was intelligent, learned, skillful in the management of men, not given to rash decisions, and there was nothing about him of the overcultivated and overcivilized aesthete. Bernal Díaz del Castillo, who saw him often and admired him this side of idolatry, detected a look of tenderness in his grave features, and this perhaps was his undoing. He had deep affections and too little cunning.

In the early years of the sixteenth century, before the coming of the Spaniards, the Aztec empire was at the height of its power and influence. Power radiated from Tenochtitlán, reaching out to the Atlantic and the Pacific, and there was scarcely

Indian dancer outside
the basilica at Guadalupe

a village or hamlet that did not pay tribute to the Emperor. But for some years there had been strange warnings and premonitions of disaster. The priests had read in the sacred books that Quetzalcóatl, the feathered serpent, would return from the East and overcome the present rulers of Mexico. Year after year there came portents and prophecies. In 1509, for example, the waters of the lake rocked violently for no apparent reason, and the temples and houses of Tenochtitlán were flooded. In 1511 a tongue of flame was seen hanging in the eastern sky, and in the same year a sanctuary on top of a pyramid caught fire and, despite desperate efforts to save it, the pyramid was consumed in the flames. In 1515 comets were seen, and these were especially bright and threatening. In the night a woman was heard screaming in a voice that could be heard all over the city: "O my sons, where shall I take you?" Most terrifying and inexplicable of all, according to the chroniclers, was the crane or egret that some fishermen found in their nets with a round mirror embedded in its skull. The bird was taken to Moctezuma, who saw or thought he saw in the mirror a vast array of men riding on deer in the direction of Tenochtitlán.

An ax would fall from the sky, a flame would descend from the heavens, the earth would open wide and engulf them. Long before the first Spaniard was seen, there was the knowledge that the gods were preparing a strange and terrible fate for the Aztecs. They could not guess how it would come about, but they knew with absolute certainty that the years of conquest were over. So they waited patiently and did not know what they were waiting for.

Toltec-Aztec pyramid, Teotihuacán

THE COMING OF CORTÉS

When he was a very old man, weighed down with the infirmities of age, blind and deaf, Bernal Díaz del Castillo dictated the last lines of his *True Chronicle of the Conquest of Mexico*. He was eighty-four, and he had spent most of his life as a magistrate in Santiago in Guatemala without ever achieving high position. He was not lacking in ambition; it was simply that ambition meant nothing to a man who had fought under Cortés, and had arrow wounds to show for it, and who had received from the hands of the Emperor Moctezuma a chieftain's daughter as a gift. He had a brood of half-Indian children and another brood of Spanish children. Through the years he had entertained them with stories of the Conquest; he knew how to tell a story well, in a dry, half-humorous manner, never laboring a point, but telling it swiftly, leaping from one episode to another.

Quite obviously, the story was taken down as he dictated it in his heavy Estremadura brogue, with no feeling for grammar or the finer artifices of prose. He would tell the story in his own way, roughly, casually, letting the sun and the air flow into it, unlike Francisco López de Gómara, the friend and secretary of Cortés, who wrote a mannered account of the Conquest based on the very words of the conqueror, though he liked to improve on Cortés and sometimes gives the impression of writing at third or fourth hand. Gómara had never been to Mexico, had no feeling for the land, and would scarcely have recognized an Indian if he saw one. Bernal Díaz wants you to see the land and the people, the beauty of the Indian cities, the flash of gunpowder, the rippling muscles of the horses, the very faces of the Indians who fought so furiously, and were so handsome, that he felt only admiration for them. He had a story to tell so strange and terrible that sometimes a strange dreamlike quality hovers over it. Then the smoke drifts away, and suddenly you find yourself in the presence of a small company of lean, hard-bitten men with red-rimmed eyes, and they are very close, and you can smell the sweat of their faces and their leather doublets.

Bernal Díaz had read the official report, and it did not please him. He felt that too much had been made of Cortés and too little of his companions-in-arms.

Toltec painted mural, Teotihuacán

35

Gómara had never fought in the wars, and Bernal Díaz had fought in a hundred and nineteen battles. So he cast his net wide, told stories about everyone he remembered, filled in the background and the foreground, and painted in all the hot, feverish colors, with the predictable result that Cortés still occupies the center of the stage, but this time he is seen in three dimensions, standing head and shoulders above everyone else, and all the more terrifying because he possesses a cool intelligence and a hot-blooded passion for destruction.

And what a man! There was no one quite like him even among the Renaissance princes. Cruel, subtle, generous, deeply religious, working in secret and ruled by his will, he marched across Mexico like an avenging angel. It was a battle of wills: one man, Cortés, against the total will of an entire nation at the very height of its civilization and its power. His soldiers were the dice he threw; all of Mexico was the prize. What he liked best of all was to enter the landscape of danger, which was familiar and precious to him. Then, with his head held high, he would survey his enemies calmly and courteously, waiting for the moment when they would destroy themselves with no more assistance than a single act of his will. He liked to put himself in his enemies' power.

The surviving portraits show a man with a broad brow, a long pointed nose, a small mouth, a firm chin under the bristling beard. His eyes were deep-set and widely spaced, and heavily lidded. Bernal Díaz says they were mild and grave, and indeed there was something priestlike about him. Remove the armor and place him in a long black gown, and he might be the rector of a religious seminary, his days spent commanding students, his nights in prayers. It was remembered that he knew many prayers by heart, gave good sermons, knew Latin well, and believed himself to be under the special protection of St. Peter. It was also remembered that in his younger days he was an inveterate gambler at dice and cards and an insatiable seducer of married women, and there was a gash in his chin, visible through his beard, to testify to a husband's displeasure. As he grew older, he gambled more recklessly, and he never lost his appetite for women.

There were so many contraries mixed up in him that the wonder is how they held together. Outwardly he seemed simple enough, very calm and composed. Tall, slender, broad-shouldered, with a fine chest and the bandy legs of a man more accustomed to ride on horseback than to walk, he presented himself to his soldiers as a soldier and nothing more. He paid strict attention to discipline, went

Toltec statue

36

the rounds every evening, visiting the soldiers' quarters and seeing that everything was in order; if he found a man without his armor, he would speak to him quietly, and if a soldier stole as much as a turkey cock, he would have him hanged. But soldiering was the least part of him. Almost he was a disembodied will, the trajectory of a thought determined to reach its target. He liked to say that God was stronger than nature—*Dios es sobre natura*—but so was the naked human will. What could be thought could always be accomplished, however improbable.

What is fascinating is the quality of his will, and how he shaped it, or it shaped him. He was himself perfectly conscious that he was guided by his will. Once he wrote to Emperor Charles V describing a particularly dangerous encounter with the Indians: "Because I was so much on my guard, they found me standing in front of their thoughts." One day the Emperor Moctezuma said pleasantly: "You must be tired after climbing up to so many temples." Cortés answered: "Neither I nor my men are ever wearied by our exertions." It was no more than the truth.

This was the man who led a pathetically small army against the island city of Tenochtitlán, with sixteen horses, a few guns, and a banner consisting of a red cross on a black ground with blue and white flames springing from the cross. He did not know—could not possibly know—what he would find at the end of the journey, yet he knew better than anyone that he would humble emperors in the dust and take possession of an empire. What he did not know, and could never have foreseen, was that the Aztecs had looked in their books of prophecies and read that the god Quetzalcóatl, the plumed serpent, who had vanished long ago from the holy city of Cholula, was about to return from his mysterious exile in the East. He would be recognized by his fair skin, long hair, and flowing black beard, unlike the beards of the Indians, which were sparse and thin; he would wear dark clothes and a dark feathered hat; and he would be armed with the attributes of divine power. Since he was the creator of the Fifth Sun, lord of creation and giver of breath, all men and all things would abase themselves before him.

The prophecy of the coming of Quetzalcóatl lies at the heart of the mystery, for without it there could have been no conquest, nor any possibility of conquest. Cortés derived his own knowledge of the prophecy gradually, over many weeks and months, and he never quite reconciled himself to playing the role of a god. That he was regarded as a god seemed to him only one more of the exasperating difficulties that confronted him, for not even the Indians who came over to the side

Aztec Calendar Stone
in the National Museum of Anthropology

of the Spaniards were able to tell him how a god behaved. They expected him to know and they watched him closely for the demonstrable signs of divinity, puzzled because he often behaved like a man. He bled when he was wounded, and sometimes he was afraid. But he possessed one thing in common with the gods, and the Indians recognized it the moment they saw him—a relentless and undeviating will. He was one of those who never turn back.

When the Aztec priests read the prophecies and spoke about the coming of a god, they were more knowledgeable than they knew, for a god did in fact accompany Cortés. He often proclaimed that he had come to bring Christ to the Indians, but Christ was rarely seen.

Although he carried the banner of the cross with the blue and white flames, this appears to have been his private banner; the army marched under the banner of the Virgin, and went into battle calling upon her for protection. While they were still preparing for the march on Tenochtitlán, they entered the coastal city of Cempoala and overthrew the idols from the high temples, but instead of erecting a statue of Christ, they erected one of the Virgin. Long afterward, whenever a ship put in at Cempoala, the Indians would run down to the shore, shouting, "Cortés! Cortés!" and "María! María!" In time the banner of the Virgin would become thoroughly familiar to the Indians, and they would remember that she was depicted crowned, with downcast eyes, in an attitude of meditation, a faint smile playing at the corners of her lips. One of the banners of the conquistadors has survived, and bears a remarkable resemblance to the Virgin of Guadalupe, the mysterious painting that appeared a few years after the Conquest on the cloak of an Indian convert. In both the banner and the miraculous painting the Virgin stands alone, without the Child.

On August 16, 1519, with the banner of the Virgin leading the way, Cortés set out on the long march to Tenochtitlán. The army climbed slowly through the low coastal hills, passing through forests of palms and banana trees, with parrots and butterflies flitting among the branches. Ahead of them lay mountains fifteen thousand feet high, scorching deserts, lava fields, landscapes of drifting cloud in which they became lost and blundered in the darkness, ravines thousands of feet deep. When they emerged from the regions of mist and rain and sudden flurries of hail, they were exhausted and in no shape to confront the biting cold winds which came down from the plateau. But they plunged on, certain that they would reach

Fragment of stone from Teotihuacán,
now in the National Museum
of Anthropology

40

Tenochtitlán, although as yet they scarcely knew the power and majesty of the city they planned to conquer. From a chieftain met during the journey they heard for the first time about the full extent of Moctezuma's possessions. "He is lord of the world," the chieftain said, "and he has thirty vassals, each of whom commands a hundred thousand warriors, and his capital is the most beautiful and strongest in the land." And when the chieftain was asked whether he knew Moctezuma, he answered: "Who does not know him? Who is there who is not his slave or his vassal?"

Moctezuma was carefully following the advance of the Spanish column through his spies. They reported that the great hounds and mastiffs ran on ahead, followed by the standard-bearer, who twirled his banner energetically, waving it backward and forward and in circles; then came the foot soldiers armed with bared swords, followed by horsemen, and these were followed by men with iron crossbows and more horsemen, and at the end of the column Cortés rode among his guards. When Moctezuma learned that Cortés was heading for Tlaxcala, one of the few cities in Mexico which refused to accept his sovereignty, he was deeply disturbed, for if the Tlaxcalans joined forces with the Spaniards, then Cortés would be able to mount a far more formidable army than he originally possessed. But like Moctezuma, the Tlaxcalans decided to test Cortés before accepting him in their midst. There were some short and savage encounters. In one of these a Tlaxcalan warrior cut off a horse's head, "reins and all," with a single blow of his sword, to the vast chagrin of Cortés, who had hoped at least that the horses would be regarded as invulnerable.

Tlaxcala proved to be the turning point, for once Cortés had established friendship with this powerful kingdom, the way was open for the advance on Tenochtitlán. Only a month had passed since he had left the coastal plains.

The next large city was Cholula, sacred to Quetzalcóatl, whose great temple stood on an immense pyramid, by far the largest of all the pyramids in Mexico. Eleven centuries had passed since Quetzalcóatl had left the city, promising to return when the time was ripe, but the Cholulans evidently believed that the time had not come, for though they treated Cortés honorably, they showed no enthusiasm for his army and obliged the Tlaxcalans to remain outside the walls while they sent messengers to Moctezuma to learn how they should treat the Spaniards. The answer was brief: Kill them. The Cholulans might have succeeded, but the strange Indian girl Ce Malinalli, a princess of Painalla in the Olmec country, who

Coatlícue, goddess of life and death, now
in the National Museum of Anthropology

acted as interpreter, discovered the plot and warned Cortés, who immediately set about to exact a terrible vengeance. At his orders there was a general massacre of the Cholulans. Torches were put to the houses, and the temple to Quetzalcóatl on the summit of the great pyramid was set on fire. When Moctezuma heard of the destruction of Cholula, he was more than ever convinced that Cortés was Quetzalcóatl, for only a god would dare to burn down his own shrine.

Altogether Cortés spent a little more than two weeks in Cholula, and then marched on toward the Lake of the Moon, taking the road between the two gigantic snow-capped volcanoes Popocatépetl and Ixtaccíhutl. From the pass the army looked down on the lake, seeing in the hazy distance the cities lying clustered on its shores and the causeways leading to Tenochtitlán itself. A stream of messengers came from Moctezuma, begging them not to enter the city, promising them immense treasures of gold if they would only return to the coast, offering to pay tribute for all eternity if only they would abandon the plan of entering the city. Cortés replied to all the messengers that he had no greater desire than to pay his respects to Moctezuma in person, and that surely at this last moment, on the eve of his entry into Tenochtitlán, this pleasure should not be denied him.

So the army marched along the causeway, with Cortés riding at the head and the Tlaxcalans taking up the rear. There, in front of them, almost within reach, as beautiful as the dawn, was the city they had dreamed about for so long. Bernal Díaz, who was among those who followed immediately behind Cortés, suddenly remembered the warnings they had received in all the cities they had passed through—how they would never escape alive once they had entered Tenochtitlán —and he wondered at the boldness of Cortés and his soldiers. "Who in all the world has ever shown such daring?" he asked. "And we—we were not even four hundred men!"

Just outside the city Moctezuma was waiting for them, arrayed in imperial panoply, under a canopy of green feathers threaded with gold and silver. He wore his richest vestments, and his feet were shod in gold sandals; so that he should not touch the earth, high officers spread their mantles before him. He came leaning on the arms of four princes. Cortés dismounted and made a reverence before the Emperor and was about to embrace him, but one of Moctezuma's officers prevented him. Yet he could not be prevented from hanging a necklace of colored beads scented with musk around Moctezuma's neck. In return Moctezuma hung around

Model of Tenochtitlán
in the National Museum of Anthropology

45

Cortés' neck two necklaces, from each of which hung eight golden shrimp. According to Francisco López de Gómara, this was a mark of special favor. It was in fact far more, for the shrimp were sacred to Quetzalcóatl, and with these two necklaces Moctezuma affirmed his belief that Cortés was indeed Quetzalcóatl, who had returned from his long and mysterious journeys to claim the empire of the Aztecs. In an extraordinary speech, which has been preserved by Bernardino de Sahagún, Moctezuma greeted Cortés as a god. He said:

> O Lord, our Lord, with what trouble, what fatigue, have you journeyed to reach us, have arrived in this land, your land, your own city of Mexico, to sit on your mat, your stool, which I have been guarding for you this while. Your vassals, the old kings, my ancestors, are gone, after they too had kept ready your mat. Would that one of them could rise from the dead and, astonished, see what my eyes truly see, for in no dream do I see your face. Ah, these days, five, ten, a string of days, I have been anxious, watching for you, waiting to see you appear from your hidden place among the clouds and mists. For the kings, my ancestors, told that you would appear, that you would return to sit on your mat, your stool. Now it has come true; you have returned. With toil, with weariness, you have reached us at last. Welcome to this land. Rest now. You are tired. Rest awhile. Rest in your palace. With your companions, the lords, take your rest.

In this fashion Cortés entered Tenochtitlán, walking on foot, being led by the Emperor. A few weeks before, in a letter to Charles V, Cortés had promised that he would make Moctezuma a vassal of the King of Spain or kill him, and now everything was coming to pass as he had hoped. Into that rich and beautiful city he came not as a conqueror but as a guest, not as a warrior but as a god. It was about noon on November 8, 1519, when he entered the enchanted city.

It had been a strange progress, and nothing was stranger than the way in which Cortés and Moctezuma calmly accepted their destiny, never questioning that their meeting had been preordained. There had been no battles between their armies, no controversies between them. Simply, quietly, with exquisite grace and tact, Moctezuma offered his empire to Cortés, and Cortés accepted it in the name of

Charles V. Many months were to pass before Charles V knew that Mexico had been added to his empire.

Meanwhile the Spaniards explored the city, marveling at the walls that were so brightly polished that they seemed to be of silver and at the flower gardens that stretched from one end of the island to the other. Moctezuma himself led them to the great market place at Tlatelolco in the northern suburbs. They wandered among the market stalls, and watched the goldsmiths and feathermakers open-mouthed with astonishment, for they had not expected to see such brilliant tapestries or such fine workmanship in gold. Then Moctezuma invited them to climb the pyramid to admire the view extending across the whole lake and far beyond: the teeming cities on the lake shore, the thousands of canoes, and the white volcanoes serenely dominating the landscape. On this pyramid the black-robed priests performed their sacrificial rites, killing their human victims by slitting open their chests with obsidian knives and offering the smoking hearts to the gods. Calmly, almost casually, Cortés turned to Moctezuma and demanded that these rites be abolished. The blood-soaked Aztec gods must be thrown down, and in their place there must be erected a statue of the Virgin. Moctezuma was distressed; he had not expected that Cortés would quarrel so soon with the ancient Aztec beliefs, and he explained quickly that such things were not possible. Cortés believed that all things were possible, and four days later he embarked on the wildest gamble of all by placing Moctezuma under arrest, forcing him at sword point to abandon his own palace and take up residence in the palace reserved for the Spaniards. For the rest of his life Moctezuma was the prisoner of Cortés.

Cortés ruled. By this sudden *coup de main* he became the Emperor of Mexico, heir to all the gold and all the jewels in the treasure house, and of all the tribute that came into the city. For six months he was able to rule quietly through an obedient Moctezuma. In May, 1520, Pedro de Alvarado, who had been appointed acting governor during the absence of Cortés, senselessly massacred some religious dancers. Cortés hurried back to Tenochtitlán to find the people in a state of rebellion and Moctezuma so appalled by the outrage that he could no longer be depended upon to defend the Spaniards. Within a month Moctezuma was dead, killed, according to the Spaniards, by a stone flung by an Indian; but according to an Indian tradition preserved by Fray Bernardino de Sahagún, he was strangled on the order of Cortés. The entire population of Tenochtitlán, enraged beyond en-

The market—woman with pottery

durance, rose against the Spaniards, who fled, losing a quarter of their horses and most of their treasure in their flight. Scarcely half the army survived.

There followed months of quiet, relentless preparation for the reconquest of the city. With a far larger Tlaxcalan army and with brigantines transported overland to ensure mastery of the lake, Cortés laid siege to Tenochtitlán, cut off its water supply—for the lake was brackish near the city—and seized control of the causeways. The Aztecs fought furiously, and elected Cuauhtémoc, the young nephew of Moctezuma, to be their new Emperor. Cuauhtémoc was no match for Cortés in guile or cunning. Slowly the city was starved into surrender while being bled to death. The cannon roared, and all night from the great plaza in Tenochtitlán there came the booming of the huge snakeskin drums. Cortés acquired a foothold on Tlatelolco, the northern part of the city, and brought up his heaviest guns and his best troops. The siege lasted seventy-five days.

Then quite suddenly it was all over, for the young Emperor was captured and the Aztecs no longer had any heart to resist. Brought before Cortés, Cuauhtémoc asked only to be killed. Cortés spoke to him pleasantly, ordered that his women should be protected, and went on to make his second ceremonial entry into Tenochtitlán. This time he did not come as a guest or as a god, but as a conqueror. Suddenly, after the confused uproar of the long siege, silence descended on the city.

That night a storm rose, the lake boiled, and ball lightning played over the great pyramid in the sacred enclosure. In the glare of the lightning Cortés surveyed his conquest. The enchanted city of the Aztecs had gone forever, and nothing remained of its former beauty. Wherever he looked he saw only the dead and the dying, ruin and devastation without end.

The Maya face

THE IMPERIAL CITY

"Muy Noble e Insigne, muy Leal e Imperial Ciudad de Mexico"—in such terms did the Spanish kings address their very noble and distinguished, very loyal and imperial city of Mexico, which was built on the ruins of Tenochtitlán. Of the nobility and distinction of the new city there were many reports, and the parchments signed with the illegible signatures of the viceroys testified to its prevailing and incessant loyalty, haughtily expressed. That it was imperial was taken as a matter of course, for had not the Aztec emperors lived there in great state, and certainly in greater state than the king of Spain? With a necessary boldness Cortés had said as much in a letter to Charles V, who seems not to have replied. All the words we associate with magnificence could be applied to Tenochtitlán. Then the Spaniards went about tearing down every vestige of that magnificence: what they built was imperial, vast, perhaps splendid, but it was not the pure perfection that had sprung out of the imagination of the unknown Aztec architects.

What happened was something that very rarely happened in Renaissance times: the whole city was laid flat. One suspects that if the Italians had conquered Tenochtitlán, they would have built around it, or a little to one side; they had an eye for the pure line, the grouping of buildings, the tensions between great monumental structures. The Aztec architects had so designed the vast square that the great double temple dominated the smaller temples and existed in a rhythmic tension with them. They were well aware of the weight and color, the subtleties and intricacies of space, for they were master builders determined to build temples worthy of the gods. But in the space of a few months all the temples of Tenochtitlán vanished. Cortés, in his third letter to Charles V, says they were destroyed, implying that the whole city was reduced to rubble in the wars, yet these temples were huge structures made of stone, and it is unlikely that they fell to the Spanish cannon or simply vanished in the flames. What is much more likely is that he ordered the Indians to destroy them, brick by brick, throwing the debris into the canals.

Maya green jade mask found in a temple at
Palenque, now at the National
Museum of Anthropology

At first he scarcely knew what to do with the ruined city. He was living in Coyoacán, uncertain whether to rebuild the city or seek another location on the lake shore. He had the power to make the decision, and it weighed heavily on him. There were a dozen places that might have been chosen, for there were at least a dozen towns around the lake. Finally, he decided that Tenochtitlán should be born again because, as he said, "it was a thing so renowned, and had been so important and memorable." He set the Indians, and his own soldiers, to work, and within four or five months a city much smaller than pre-Conquest Tenochtitlán arose. He wrote to the Emperor:

> In the four or five months since we began to rebuild the city, it is already very beautiful, and Your Majesty may believe that it grows nobler every day. As once it was the head and mistress of these provinces, so it will be again. We have built and will continue to build it in such a way that the Spaniards will be perfectly strong and safe, supreme lords over the Indians, secure from any fear of being attacked by them.

The new city was therefore a fortress designed to hold the Indians in subjection. According to the chronicler known as the Anonymous Conquistador, writing about ten years after the Conquest, the houses were built of heavy blocks of stone, and each house was a strong point that could be defended on all sides. The houses were all the same height and looked very much the same, except for a few that were provided with turrets. There were four hundred houses arranged in sixteen blocks around the Plaza Mayor. The city of Cortés must have looked like a military cantonment—harsh, utilitarian, ugly. Of Spanish *grandeza* there was no trace. The time of ornamentation would come later, when the Spaniards felt more secure.

The Indians were not the only dangerous element. Floods, subsidence, the torrential rains of summer threatened to sweep the small capital away; and although the first severe floods did not occur until thirty years after the Conquest, there were periodic warnings even during the early years of occupation. A pestilence, which appears to have been a peculiarly virulent form of smallpox, made havoc of the Indians and carried off many of the conquistadors. It was not an ordinary epidemic sweeping away a few thousands of people, but one that raged like a prairie fire, burning out whole villages, whole tribes. The safety of the new city

A fighter and his bull

55

was assured, because the defeated Indians were too weak to go on fighting. The conquerors were less destructive than the pestilence.

Though the Aztecs had been conquered, there was still the danger that some of the unconquered tribes of the interior might march on the city. The work of building fortifications went on at a breakneck pace, with the Indians set to forced labor. We hear of Indian laborers toppling from the roofs and being dashed to the ground, of others who were smothered by falling walls, and of many who died because hard labor reduced their resistance to disease. Mexico City was built on a foundation of Indian bones.

Cortés was determined to build the city quickly because he wanted to secure his power and also because he wanted to restore peace to the land, so that it would be once more wealthy and productive. He built a dockyard, where the ships which had taken part in the final conquest were on permanent display, and where new ships were continually being built, since it was necessary that the Spaniards should remain masters of the lake. Around the walls of the city all the approaches were cleared, so that the guns of the fortress dominated the landscape. Seventy cast-iron guns were mounted on the walls. The guns were homemade, for a vein of iron had been found in Taxco. Cortés also cast five bronze guns; copper was abundant, and a small amount of tin had been found in Taxco, although it was so expensive to mine that it cost as much as silver. There was no difficulty in making stone balls, and powder was provided by mixing niter, which was readily available, with sulphur from the neighboring volcanoes. Cortés was especially pleased that everything he needed was being provided by the soil of Mexico.

His own palace was built of hewn stone, but it was provided with wooden floors and wooden beams, and thus resembled the palace of Moctezuma. It was said that seven thousand cedar beams were employed in the construction of his palace, and Bernal Díaz, who liked simplicity, complained that there were so many courtyards that he was always getting lost in them. "It was," he said, "like being in the labyrinth at Crete."

Within a few years two thousand families were living within the walled city, and Cortés could congratulate himself that all danger was over. He advanced money to the conquistadors to bring their wives from Spain, and there was a special fund for arranging the passage of young women. From Cuba, Santo Domingo, and Jamaica came horses, cows, sheep, goats, and pigs, for there was a great need

Pottery market

57

for draft horses, milk, wool, hides, and meat. From the islands, too, came sugar cane, mulberry trees, and vines, and from Spain came olives and nuts. Even without the imports from Spain and the islands the city was well provisioned, for every morning at daybreak the Indians would race in their canoes across the lake to sell provisions to the fortress city. The Spaniards were still heavily outnumbered, for there were thirty thousand families of Indians living in nearby Tlatelolco and uncounted thousands in the other towns around the lake. But the domination of the Spaniards was absolute, and they had little fear of invasion. Missionaries were fanning over the country, and the Indians were becoming fervent converts to the faith.

By converting the Indians, establishing schools, and building churches on the sites of Aztec temples, the missionaries succeeded in dominating the conquered people. Church and state ruled together, and more than one viceroy was also an archbishop. The friars were closest to the people, and there grew up a whole generation of priests who spoke better Náhuatl than Spanish. Bernardino de Sahagún, a wise and venerable Franciscan friar, was so devoted to the Indians that he collected their songs and legends and wrote a voluminous account of Aztec history. He lived in great simplicity, but other friars lived in great luxury. In Mexico City the conventual houses expanded into great palaces, which threatened to spill over into the highways, with the result that special laws had to be passed to limit their size. *Grandeza*, the earthly magnificence which the world associated with kings, became habitual among the abbots who lived in greater splendor than the viceroys.

The abbots ate off gold plates and were attended by jeweled blackamoors and as many female servants as they pleased. Luxury became the commonplace; frugality was set aside, for it impeded men's devotions. The riches pouring into the Church served to glorify both Christ and abbot. In the massive golden altars of the Church of San Francisco Javier at Tepotzotlán, some thirty miles from Mexico City, we can still see the barbaric splendor of the Church in the Golden Age. Most of the church treasures vanished in the revolutions, but this church has been accorded a special immunity, having been converted into a museum. There, finally, in those towering sheets of intricately carved gold, or, rather, of gilded wood, the dreams of the conquistadors become reality, the world vanishes, and only gold remains.

It is a staggering exhibition of the goldsmith's art, for one expects gold to be

Chamula Indian boys in the countryside

treated with a certain reticence, a certain sense of propriety. Gold, we tell our-selves, is for finger rings and small ornaments, and not to be plastered thickly over whole walls. At Tepotzotlán the entire church—the floors, the walls, the ceiling—is thickly encrusted with gold. There are so many garlands of gold flowers, so many clusters of gold grapes, so many gold saints peeping out of their gold-encrusted caves; there is such a parade of gold ornamentation and encrustation without apparent focus that the eye loses all hope of finding a resting place and abandons the struggle in despair. Here and there, amid the gold curlicues, a Christ painted in vivid flesh colors emerges out of a gold box supported by gold angels and cherubs. He startles for a moment, but the sudden intrusion of flesh colors is so out of place and so unexpected that there is a tendency to dismiss him as an interloper. He has no business in the gold church. Indeed, there is very little space for him, and, accordingly, he is represented kneeling, dragging his cross behind him. He is unconvincing, whereas the gold walls are only too convincing, even if they say nothing at all except that an immense treasure has been expended upon the church.

Gold spins and spurts, and the saints are drowned in it. There are sheets of pure gold, and gold so fretted and clotted that it is beyond belief that there was any original design. The Indians who worked on the interior of the church appear to have surrendered to a happy frenzy, and all the golden angels have recognizably Indian features. The churches in Mexico City have a barren look, for all the gold has been stripped from them, but once they, too, were decked out in golden colors. Thomas Gage, the English Dominican friar who visited Mexico City in 1625, speaks of "roofs and beams daubed with gold" and "tabernacles for several saints richly wrought in gold, so that twenty thousand ducats is a common price for many of them." He regarded Mexico City as El Dorado, and thought it fit for the flames.

Meanwhile, for he was an aristocratic Englishman with worldly tastes as well as a Dominican friar, he enjoyed his visit, engaged in various extracurricular affairs, and was especially attracted by the appearance of the gold- and silver-plated coaches, which were more splendid than any coaches he had seen in Europe. In his book, which he called *The English-American, his travail by sea and land, or a New Survey of the West Indies,* he wrote:

> In my time it was thought to be of between thirty and forty thousand inhabitants, who are so proud and rich that half the city was judged to keep coaches, for it was a most credible report that in Mexico in my time

Indian seller

there were above fifteen thousand coaches. It is a by-word that at Mexico there are four things fair, that is to say, the women, the apparel, the horses, and the streets. But to his I may add the beauty of some of the coaches of the gentry, which do exceed in cost the best of the Court of Madrid and other parts of Christendom; for there they spare no silver, nor gold, nor precious stones, nor cloth of gold, nor the best silks from China to enrich them. And to the gallantry of their horses the pride of some doth add the cost of bridles and shoes of silver.

The streets of Christendom must not compare with those in breadth and cleanness, but especially in the riches of the shops which do adorn them. Above all, the goldsmiths' shops and works are to be admired. The Indians, and the people of China that have been made Christians and every year come hither, have perfected the Spaniards in that trade. The Viceroy that went thither the year 1625 caused a popinjay to be made of silver, gold and precious stones with the perfect colours of the popinjay's feathers (a bird bigger than a pheasant), with such exquisite art and perfection, to present unto the King of Spain, that it was prized to be worth in riches and workmanship half a million of ducats. There is in the cloister of the Dominicans a lamp hanging in the church with three hundred branches wrought in silver to hold so many candles, besides a hundred little lamps for oil set in it, every one being made with several workmanship so exquisitely that it is valued to be worth four hundred thousand ducats; and with such-like curious works are many streets made more rich and beautiful from the shops of goldsmiths.

Both men and women are excessive in their apparel, using more silks than stuffs and cloth. Precious stones and pearls further much this their vain ostentation; a hat-band and rose made of diamonds in a gentleman's hat is common, and a hat-band of pearls is ordinary in a tradesman; nay a blackamoor or tawny young maid and slave will make hard shift but she will be in fashion with her neck-chain and bracelets of pearls, and her ear-bobs of some considerable jewels. The attire of this baser sort of people of blackamoors and mulattoes (which

Mitla, Mixtec archaeological site,
with colonial church built with stones
from one of Mitla's temples

are of a mixed nature, of Spaniards and blackamoors) is so light, and their carriage so enticing, that many Spaniards even of the better sort (who are too prone to venery) disdain their wives for them.

Thomas Gage particularly enjoyed the spectacle of the Negro and mestizo girls on parade, describing their clothes in great detail—the silk petticoats, the holland sleeves, the ribbons and laces, the girdles of pearl, and the knots of gold. He noted that "their bare, black, and tawny breasts are covered with bobs hanging from their chains of pearls," and that they played inviting games with their shawls, revealing their luxuriant flesh, so that they were "more like roaring boys than honest civil maids." They wore high, silver-plated shoes and carried themselves with the air of conquerors. They were, he thought, among the wickedest creatures who ever set foot on the earth, but he could not take his eyes away from them.

Nothing surprised him more than the wanton glances of these young women, who behaved as though all Mexico City belonged to them. They were the mistresses of the Spaniards, and had earned their freedom. Luxury, at first enjoyed only by the conquistadors, had now descended among the ranks of slaves and former slaves, who took it in their stride. He watched these women eagerly, and noted that they were rapidly changing the complexion of the city. The former slaves were also acquiring political power and threatening the security of the state. "There are so many of this kind both men and women grown to a height of pride and vanity, that many times the Spaniards have feared they would rise up and mutiny against them." And in fact, later in the century, there were many uprisings and rebellions, and the viceroy was accustomed to the cry: "Death to the *gachupines*! Death to the Spaniards!" More than one viceroy was run out of the country as the result of a popular uprising. By the time the revolution finally broke out, Mexico had become largely a mestizo country. The revolutionaries bore Spanish names, but they were descended from the Indians and the Negroes whom the conquistadors had enslaved.

Thomas Gage had an eye, too, for the young gallants who paraded as they still do, in Alameda Park, though they can no longer drive through the park in their golden coaches. The ancient elegance has departed; the people who stroll there today are the common people of the city, more intent on reading the newspapers in the shade than in carousing. Thomas Gage had a passion for elegance, and describes the elegant costumes worn by the actors in the drama:

Sunday family outing in Chapultepec Park

The gallants of this city shew themselves daily, some on horseback, and most in coaches, about four of the clock in the afternoon in a pleasant shady field called *la Alameda*, full of trees and walks, somewhat like unto our Moorfields, where do meet as constantly as the merchants upon our exchange about two thousand coaches, full of gallants, ladies, and citizens, to see and to be seen, to court and to be courted, the gentlemen having their train of blackamoor slaves some a dozen, some half a dozen waiting on them, in brave and gallant liveries, heavy with gold and silver lace, with silk stockings on their black legs, and roses on their feet, and swords by their sides; the ladies also carry their train by their coach's side of such jet-like damsels as before have been mentioned for their light apparel, who with their bravery and white mantles over them seem to be, as the Spaniard saith, *mosca en leche*, a fly in milk. But the train of the Viceroy who often goeth to this place is wonderful stately, which some say is as great as the train of his master the King of Spain.

The blackamoors have gone, and so have the ancient liveries, and the park is still "a pleasant shady field" where the lovers stroll and the band plays on Thursday evenings. Thomas Gage forgot to say that one end of the park was a private preserve of the Church and was known as *el Quemadero*, the place of burning, where the victims of the Inquisition were burned at the stake. It was an odd omission, for he was a Dominican friar, and the Dominicans had a special interest in inquisitions.

Today the old imperial city still stands, shorn of its former grandeur. There are only a few palaces owned by the descendants of the ancient Spanish nobility, whose resounding names were once uttered in whispers. The great blue-tiled and heavily ornamented palace which once belonged to the Count del Valle de Orizaba has become a drugstore, and the palace of the Count de Santiago de Calimaya has become a museum. Others have become schools, shops, offices, government buildings, warehouses. You recognize them by their sumptuously carved stonework and by their heavily barred windows; by daylight they have a down-at-heel appearance, but in moonlight they come into their own, for the Churrigueresque decorations catch the moonbeams and they look best in the pale wash of silver. The palaces were built like fortresses and were intended to inspire respect and fear. Now they owe what little life remains in them to the mercies of the moon.

Left
Flower market, Xochimilco

Next two pages
Floating gardens, Xochimilco

THE VICEROYS

You can see the viceroys in Chapultepec Castle in the long galleries especially reserved for them—those dark and solemn men with beady eyes and pursed lips, clothed in the austere black silk of Spain, sagging under the weight of their ribbons and decorations, and on their faces there is all the melancholy of overworked accountants. The paintings are flaking away and the brown varnish is threatening to obliterate them entirely. They are all there, all sixty-one of them, and often they are known by their numbers—historians will speak of Virrey XXXVIII or Virrey XLI—as though they were milestones or the numbers of pages. For three hundred years they ruled New Spain, and very few of them are memorable.

The first viceroy was Don Antonio de Mendoza, who arrived in Mexico City in November, 1535. "The most illustrious and good Knight and worthy of high memory Don Antonio" came from one of the most aristocratic families in Spain, his father having been the captain general of the forces that invested Granada. He had been ambassador to Hungary and was learned in all the ways of the court. He looked as lean and hungry as a hawk, but he was, in fact, a superbly talented administrator, with a special gift for destroying his enemies. His task was to conquer the conquerors: to reduce Cortés to absolute obedience and to assume complete control of New Spain in the name of the King. Pestilences raged, there were armed uprisings, the Negro slaves and the Chichimec Indians revolted, expeditions were sent out to California, New Mexico, and the Philippines, and there were bitter quarrels about the ownership of land and whether the Indians should be treated as slaves; and all the while the stern, unsmiling man in the viceregal palace was in complete command, coolly arranging the pieces on the chessboard, never at a loss for that final and irrevocable move which would sweep his enemies off the board.

At the beginning the people of Mexico City had hoped for someone more colorful. When he arrived in a carriage led by a team of snow-white horses, wearing the royal livery and attended by his own viceregal guards, the city exploded

Christmas tree decorations
in Alameda Park

70

in a fiesta of joy. There were carnivals and jousting bouts, parades across the Plaza Mayor, concerts, free food for the people. Cortés had been a severe ruler, acting by whim, striding about the city as though he owned it, and indeed he did own most of it. It was hoped that Mendoza would be gentler, or at least more predictable. He smiled, he nodded pleasantly, and from time to time there would come another stern law or another harsh stricture on the conquistadors. He outmaneuvered Cortés, who returned to Spain to plead his cause only to find that the court, though disposed to honor him and grant him a vast estate larger than all Spain and the titles of Marqués del Valle and Captain General of New Spain, preferred to leave him with only the empty and intangible perquisites of power. Cortés was given a most beautiful coat of arms: it bore the black double-headed eagle of the Holy Roman Empire, a golden lion, three gold crowns, the city of Mexico, and around it there were arranged seven crowned heads representing the seven kings he claimed to have conquered. No one else could claim so august an insigne. He was the king of kings, lord of Mexico, emperor of a vast territory stretching from Cuernavaca to Guatemala; and he was eating out his heart in Spain, dreaming of the great days when he was destroying an empire single-handed. Quietly, patiently, Mendoza had clipped his claws.

In 1548, toward the end of Mendoza's long reign, Juan de Tolosa discovered the rich silver mines in Zacatecas. Within a few months the color of Mexico City changed; everything was silver. Wealth poured into the city and into the ports, and more than ever it became the task of the viceroy to act as the chief accountant, seeing that every ounce of silver was accounted for. When he left Mexico three years later to become the viceroy of Peru, Mendoza was already dying, worn out by his exertions. He had left his stamp on the country, and henceforth the stern bureaucrats, modeling themselves on the first viceroy, would rule. None of the sixty viceroys who followed was his equal.

Sometimes there came a viceroy with human sympathies. In an unlikely period, in the full decadence of Spanish rule with a dissolute playboy on the throne, there came the young Marqués de Mancera, a good horseman, a hard drinker, and an efficient administrator. He had married the beautiful and aristocratic Doña Leonor Carreto, who enjoyed poetry and painting as much as her husband enjoyed the company of the hard-drinking gallants of the city. Since they were both young and determined to enjoy themselves, they broke with convention, threw down the

Paper flower market

barriers that separated the palace from the people, and celebrated fiestas on every permissible occasion. The Marquesa opened a literary salon and invited all the young aristocrats to attend, and soon it became fashionable to be young, to dance, to write poetry, collect books, and discuss the affairs of the day openly and sensibly. The Marqués shocked the sensibilities of the landowners by forbidding physical punishment of Indians and Negroes even when they were captured after coming out in open revolt.

One of the young women who attended the vicereine's literary salon was Juana Inés de Asbaje y Ramírez de Santillana, who came from a rich Spanish family long resident in New Spain. She was beautiful and precociously intelligent, deeply religious and determinedly unconventional. They said she read at the age of three, and before she was ten she had mastered Latin after twenty lessons. At fifteen she was writing secular and religious poetry, and at twenty she delighted the viceroy by attacking the professors at the University, playing the academic game of quoting the most learned authorities with the proper scholarly air. She was always falling in and out of love, and in moods of despair she would write mystical verses about death. Life, she wrote, *"es cadáver, es polvo, es sombra, es nada."* Life is a cadaver, is dust, is shadow, is nothing. In her attitude to death she was characteristically Mexican, but cheerfulness kept breaking through, and she continued to write passionate verses that appear to have been directed to the other ladies of honor in the vicereine's court. Suddenly she abandoned the court, gave her estates to the poor, took the veil, and retired with a library of four thousand books to the convent of San Jeronimo, where she continued to write brilliantly, held a court of her own, and refused to obey her superiors who insisted that she should spend more time at her devotions. She was no longer Juana Inés de Asbaje. She had become Sor Juana Inés de la Cruz.

She was painted in her well-furnished cell, wearing a long white silken gown and a black hood, sitting dramatically beside a table draped in royal scarlet, with row upon row of books behind her. It is one of the few good paintings made in viceregal times. Pale, beautiful, superbly in command of herself, she gazes out of the painting with the air of someone who is faintly surprised and amused to find herself so beautiful, so elegant, and so devout. She has the pure and classic beauty of the well-born Castilian, and described herself when she wrote in one of her most famous poems:

Detail from an old *hacienda*

74

Rosa divina, que en gentil cultura
eres, con tu fragrante sutileza,
magisterio purpúreo en la belleza,
enseñanza nevada a la hermosura.

Amago de la humana arquitectura,
ejemplo de la vana gentileza,
en cuyo sér unió naturaleza
la cuna alegre y triste sepultura.

Divine rose, who in gentle breeding
are with your subtle fragrance
the royal mastery of beauty,
a snow-white lesson in loveliness.

Image of human architecture,
example of a vain gentleness,
in whose being nature has united
the joyous cradle and the joyless sepulcher.

So she wrote in one of those very precious poems designed to prove the vanity of all things, demanding of herself that she should cast her beauty aside as a flower casts its petals, since beauty vanishes and death conquers all. These poems are never quite convincing; she was in love with life even if she was in love with death.

As she grew older and her beauty faded, a change came over her. Quite suddenly, at the age of thirty-eight, a crisis came to her life, and she turned away from poetry to the contemplation of God. She gave away her rich library, composed a confession of faith, which she signed with her own blood, and took to extreme acts of penance and self-chastisement. The elegant and devout Sor Juana Inés de la Cruz vanished into the anonymity of prayer. She loved the sisters in the convent just as tenderly as before, but now her love was silent and undemanding. When an epidemic swept through Mexico City, she gave herself up to nursing them with an absolute devotion. She had studied medicine and knew what had to be done. In a few days she caught the infection and died, on April 17, 1695. She was the greatest of the Mexican poets, and it was remembered that she was also the most beautiful.

The market—an old Indian

None of the viceroys who followed the young Marqués de Mancera had his human qualities, and only one is remembered with affection by Mexicans today. This was Juan Vicente de Güemes Pacheco de Padilla Horcasitas y Aguayo, Count of Revillagigedo, the fifty-second viceroy, who reigned from 1789 to 1794. The awesome length of his name reflects the age he lived in, when names were more important than acts. His portrait in the Gallery of Viceroys at Chapultepec Castle shows a man with clean-cut features and a jutting chin. He looks like Thomas Jefferson, his contemporary, and he had much of Jefferson's wide-ranging spirit of inquiry.

Juan Vicente had many advantages over his predecessors. He did not come fresh-minted from Spain with no knowledge of the country he was sent to rule. As a young man he served as captain of the Viceregal Guard under his father, the first Count of Revillagigedo and the forty-first viceroy. The old Count was a gruff martinet, who liked order and discipline and could be very harsh when the occasion demanded. His son had a lighter hand.

Juan Vicente returned to Spain, pursued a military career, commanded the Gibraltar Guard, and might have remained a soldier for the rest of his life if it had not occurred to Charles III, the wisest of the Spanish Bourbon kings, to send to Mexico City someone who really knew the country, for it was abundantly clear that a succession of incompetent viceroys had brought it close to ruin. In Juan Vicente he found exactly the man he needed. Soon after making the appointment, the King died, leaving his kingdom to his half-imbecile second son, Charles IV, the last and least of his line.

When Juan Vicente reached Mexico City, the people broke out in a pandemonium of joy. A painting of the inaugural procession has survived. The viceroy's carriage winds through the crowded streets, where banners wave and women throw flowers. But the city is falling into ruins; hucksters' booths lean against the walls of the viceregal palace; there is an air of decay and abandonment. Writing about this time the journalist Carlos María Bustamente described the city as "a cesspool, filthy and pestiferous." From his window the new viceroy looked out on a filthy market place, littered with refuse, a stench rising from open sewers; and there were more booths in the courtyards of his own palace. There were no police, no night watchmen, no street lights. Shortly after he took office, there was an appalling murder. Eleven people had been killed under mysterious circumstances. Like a

modern detective he solved the murder, brought the criminals to justice, and then set about bringing justice to the city.

During the five years of his reign he poured a new life and energy into the city. He worked prodigiously; it was said that he went to bed at nine o'clock and rose at one o'clock, studying documents through the night. He organized a system of night watchmen, established a police force, founded a fire brigade, paved the streets, set up street lamps, filled up the open sewers, closed down the graveyards, and ordered that henceforth there should be no cemeteries within the city. In one of the palace courtyards he set up a suggestion box, and anyone could complain to him without fear of reprisal. There was scarcely any department of government that did not feel the sharp impress of his mind. Records had been kept chaotically. He ordered that all the viceregal and military documents should be properly labeled and kept in such a way that they could be found at a moment's notice. He trained archivists, and went on to train teachers in the schools he founded, for he was the first in Mexico to establish free primary education. For the poor he provided clothes, and for foundlings he established a hospital, insisting that they should be regarded as fully legitimate.

The wealth of Mexico came from her mines. He rebuilt and re-equipped the School of Mines and saw that it was provided with a suitable faculty. Like Jefferson, he was passionately interested in botany and vigorously promoted botanical studies; and if any new flower or plant was discovered, he asked that it should be sent at once to the palace. He was deeply interested in ancient Aztec history, which few viceroys had ever studied. He built aqueducts, baths, and fountains; the Alameda, the beautiful park in the center of the city, is largely his creation. He built highways where previously there were only mule tracks, and he outfitted a fleet to explore the north Pacific and another to patrol the coasts. He completed the façade of the Cathedral, which had been begun more than two hundred years before. During his reign, in 1790, the Aztec calendar stone and the giant statue of Coatlícue were discovered near the Cathedral.

He did all these things with a kind of casual grace, sweet-tempered and fearless. As a loyal subject of the King, he arrested and punished people who, influenced by the American and French revolutions, protested the Viceroy's benevolent despotism, preferring the chaos of revolution. He had many enemies, for he trod on many toes and was especially energetic in his dealing with corrupt officials. Yet

Market scene

in Spain he was regarded with respect, for during his reign the Crown revenues reached their highest point in history.

He may have known that he would have only a short reign. Power had passed into the hands of the former guardsman Manuel de Godoy, the plump lover of the sickly, blue-lipped Queen María Luisa. Charles IV, who preferred shooting pheasants to anything else, connived at the Queen's infidelities. He took no interest in New Spain, and when Godoy insisted on making one of his own creatures the viceroy, the King had no objections. Juan Vicente was recalled in 1794. For the guidance of his successor, who had the impressive name of Miguel de la Grúa Talamanca, Marqués de Branciforte, he wrote an *Instrucción Reservada*, or Confidential Advice, in which he demonstrated by precept and example the proper way to govern an empire, stressing the importance of reforms, and of kindliness and courtesy. The Marqués de Branciforte was supremely uninterested. Like his master, he was vain, corrupt, youthful, and sinister. His aim was to make a colossal fortune by ingratiating himself with his masters. Just as the best of the Spanish Bourbon kings was followed by the worst, so the best of the viceroys was followed by the worst. The Marqués made his fortune, and four years later he returned to Spain.

There are no statues to Juan Vicente in Mexico City. There is, however, an impressive statue of Charles IV, a gift to the city from the time-serving Marqués de Branciforte. The heroic equestrian portrait was designed by Don Manuel Tolsá, the brilliant director of sculpture in the Academy of San Carlos, and there is not the least doubt that it is the finest equestrian statue in the New World. The horse and rider were cast in a single piece, and weigh thirty tons. The horse is magnificently monumental, with a powerful chest and wonderfully curving rump, majestically at ease. A Caesar or a Tamerlane, riding in triumph through conquered cities, would choose such a horse. At the very least the rider should have the features of a second-class sergeant. Unfortunately, the rider has the features of Charles IV. It is the same insipid face which peers out of Goya's painting "King Charles IV and His Family," in which the King advances into the foreground by placing one foot delicately before the other and seems about to overbalance as the result of an excessive exertion.

Poor Charles! Goya pinned him down neatly, as though he were an obese butterfly, and the Mexican sculptor has done the same. He wears a swelling toga, an enormous laurel wreath presses down on his brow, and he proudly extends an

Saturday at the village fish market

improbable field marshal's baton in his outstretched hand, but there is no disguising a fat little shopkeeper. The portrait, as it finally emerged, was as merciless as Goya's.

In 1802 the great equestrian statue was set up in the center of the vast square facing the Cathedral. There was an ornate pedestal, and in addition, to mark the singular beauty of the statue and the importance of the King, a low balustrade in the shape of a circle was built around it. The balustrade enclosed the greater part of the square, and there were four ornamental gates, each guarded by soldiers in sentry boxes, through which those who wished to pay their respects to the statue might enter. The gates were usually locked, and a special dispensation from the viceregal palace was needed to open them.

There he stood in the center of a vast circle paved in glaring white stone, alone and unapproachable except by those who were especially favored. The Cathedral served as a backdrop, the viceregal palace and the courts of justice kept watch over him; and his shadow, moving around the circle, marked out the hours. The august majesty and the loneliness of kingship had never before been expressed so wonderfully in bronze.

He did not stay there very long. At eleven o'clock on the night of September 16, 1810, Father Miguel Hidalgo y Costilla, a Spanish Roman Catholic priest, signaled the beginning of the revolt against Spain by ringing the church bell, crying out: "Long live Our Lady of Guadalupe! Long live Independence!" Within a week he had an army of fifty thousand men. From Dolores, where the revolution began, the army marched on Mexico City, destroying everything in its path, only to be destroyed in its turn by the army of the viceroy. Hidalgo was captured, condemned for heresy and other crimes by an ecclesiastical court, given over to the secular arm, and shot by a firing squad nine months after he had raised the standard of revolt. But the revolution was only beginning. Another priest, José María Morelos, continued the struggle until he fell in the viceroy's hands and was executed in 1815. Six years later a revolutionary adventurer, Agustín de Iturbide, took the capital and proclaimed himself Emperor of a free and independent Mexico, while the sixty-first viceroy, who bore the surprising name of Juan O'Donohú, sailed sadly for Spain.

Mexico was at last free of Spain, but the men who fought for Mexican freedom had not counted upon losing their freedom to an Emperor, and the brief reign of

The market—a hat of garlic

Agustín I was not marked by universal rejoicing. Carrying a scepter and wearing an ermine gown, the Empress beside him, he marched in a stately procession across the Zócalo to be crowned in the Cathedral, and on that day there was no sign of the statue of Charles IV. Instead of removing the statue, the new Emperor simply boarded it up with a huge wooden globe painted blue. Exactly what the blue globe represented was not clear: perhaps the earth, perhaps the heavens. There it remained until the Mexicans grew tired of their Emperor and expelled him from the country, threatening to shoot him if he ever returned. He did return, and the Mexicans very sensibly put him up against a wall and shot him. His last words before the firing squad took aim were properly memorable. "Fellow Mexicans," he said, "I recommend to you in the moment of my death that you should love our country and observe our holy religion. I die for having returned to help you, and I die happy, for I die among you." He had reigned for nine months.

There remained the question of what should be done with the bronze statue which reposed in its blue, egglike coffin. There it stood at the very heart of the city, majestic and invisible. Since these were revolutionary times, it was decided to remove the statue to a graveyard. This was a fitting ending for the King, who was thus ceremonially buried. The statue might have remained forever in some abandoned corner of the graveyard, sinking deeper and deeper into the earth, if it had not occurred to some professors at the University that it deserved a better fate. It could not, of course, go back to the Zócalo, or to any of the other plazas in Mexico City, but surely some secure and sheltered place could be found for it. They reasoned that posterity should have the pleasure of gazing on a statue which in the eyes of Alexander von Humboldt was second only to the equestrian statue of Marcus Aurelius in Rome. The University took possession of it, and it was erected in the decent obscurity of a small corner of the University cloisters.

In 1852 the statue found its fourth resting place. Times had changed. There was no longer any deep feeling for or against Charles IV, who had vanished quietly into one of those potholes that litter the roads of history. He could be safely disinterred and set up a little way beyond Alameda Park, in what were then the outskirts of the city. The city caught up with him and flowed round him, and today the statue occupies a place of eminence at the intersection of the Avenida Juárez and the Paseo de la Reforma. In this splendid setting Charles IV dominates the main artery of the city as previously he had dominated the Zócalo.

Open-air vegetable market

The Mexicans have a great affection for the horse, and none for the rider. They call it *el Caballito*, "the little horse," in affectionate tribute to its enormous size, and they are inclined to forget the presence of the fat little King. In their eyes the King scarcely exists, being no more than a necessary decorative trimming. They rarely pause to read the bronze inscription on the pedestal, written in the resounding rhetoric that always accompanies the sunset splendors of an imperial age:

> *The Viceroy Don Miguel de la Grúa Talamanca, Marqués de Branciforte, governed New Spain from 1794 to 1798, and caused to be made this statue of Charles IV of the House of Bourbon, King of Spain and the Indies. It was erected in the Plaza Mayor of Mexico December 9, 1803, on the birthday of the Queen María Luisa in the reign of the Viceroy Don José de Iturrigaray.*

It was a happy touch to remember the birthday of Queen María Luisa, and no doubt this was done to give pleasure to her lover, Manuel Godoy, the real ruler of Spain. A censorious Mexican government, disapproving of kings, queens, and viceroys, added a further sentence to the inscription on the pedestal: *"México la conserva como un monumento de arte."* There is the implication that the King is merely tolerated, and if the statue had been cast in two pieces he would long ago have been removed.

Poor Charles! But also, and more emphatically, lucky Charles! There are no statues of Cortés or Moctezuma, none of the Count of Revillagigedo; and all the other viceroys are unremembered, and all the other kings of Spain are forgotten. But Charles remains—happy, bumbling, lethargic Charles, who did no good to anyone, has the place of honor. Lucky Charles, to be immortalized by Goya and by Tolsá! Despised and forgotten, he still rules over the city; and neither the exhaust fumes of the automobiles nor the shadows of the skyscrapers which cluster around him can take away from him an inch of his glory.

The market—vegetables

JUÁREZ
AND MAXIMILIAN

After the viceroys came the revolutionaries—so many of them, over so long a period, that Mexico was often in danger of being destroyed by them. The nineteenth century was a period of revolutionary turmoil, which did not come to an end until Porfirio Díaz seized power in 1876 and went on to rule his exhausted country for thirty-five years as an absolute dictator. But it was not Porfirio Díaz whom the Mexicans remember with gratitude. The man they remember was a full-blooded Zapotec Indian from Oaxaca, who did not learn Spanish until he was fifteen years old. As a boy he was a shepherd in the hills near Monte Albán, and he might have died a shepherd if someone had not detected gleams of intelligence in him and sent him to a theological seminary in the hope of making a good priest out of him. Instead, he became a lawyer, and later governor of Oaxaca, and finally president of Mexico. His name was Benito Juárez, and the Mexicans have the same feeling for him that the Americans have for Abraham Lincoln.

There was nothing remarkable about his person. He was short, thickset, dark-skinned, with the stern, unsmiling features of a country schoolmaster beset with intractable and quarrelsome pupils. He never felt the need to appeal to the gallery. He had no gift for speechmaking, and he wrote a heavy-handed prose based on Justinian's *Pandects*. Colorless and cautious, he was the greatest revolutionary of them all, for he possessed something which is very rare at all times, and was especially rare in the Mexico of his time—he possessed a sense of absolute justice, as some musicians possess absolute pitch. He acted throughout his life as though Justice stood by his side.

In the National Palace you can still see the rooms where he lived throughout his three terms as president. His bed, his furniture, his razors, his shaving mug, his clothes, his handkerchiefs, all the small memorabilia of his life have been piously preserved. The faded daguerreotype photographs hang on the walls, and he gazes out of them with a calm despondency, a stern despair. In one of these rooms on

Colonial arcade

the ground floor of the palace he died of angina pectoris. In the last hours of his life the doctors poured boiling water over his chest in the hope of putting an end to the agonizing pain. It was a strange remedy, and he died with his chest scalded and bloated, screaming with pain. Justice had deserted him at the last.

Just as Cortés believed himself called upon to put an end to the Aztec empire in the name of the Virgin, so Juárez, who was also deeply religious, felt he had been called to put an end to the ruling powers of Mexico in the name of justice. The ruling powers were the Church, the landowners with their vast *haciendas*, the bureaucrats who continued to rule as though they had received a dispensation from the Spanish king to exercise power in perpetuity. The Church owned half the wealth of the country, the *hacendados* owned the remaining half. The Indians had been dispossessed, and over the centuries there had come the Indian cry: *"Ni tlaca!"* "We also are human!" In this cry Juárez recognized the plea for human justice, and as constitutional president, with a bankrupt treasury, he set about his great program of reforms, which was never to be completely implemented. The Constitution of 1857 had given the government the power to confiscate the church lands and to abolish the special privileges of the Church and of the Army, to authorize civil marriages, and to provide for government schools. The inevitable consequence was open warfare between the Church and the State, and there were long periods when the State consisted only of Juárez riding across the country in his famous black carriage, the state documents lying in a box at his feet or in his top hat, a fugitive always in danger of being arrested and put up against a wall by the local *hacendados* through whose territory he passed.

In the museum at Chapultepec Castle you can see the black carriage, so strong, so sturdy, and so unpretentious—just such a carriage as a country doctor might use when making his rounds—and it seems to be an abstract portrait of Juárez himself. Beside it there has been set quite deliberately the delicately gilded and ornate carriage of the Emperor Maximilian, the young brother of Franz Josef of Austria, who accepted the throne of Mexico at the prompting of Napoleon III and at the invitation of the leading *hacendados* and bishops of the time. Mexico had a President and an Emperor.

On June 12, 1864, Maximilian and his Belgian wife Carlota made their state entry into Mexico City and were crowned in the Cathedral. Maximilian was thirty-one, tall, elegant, cultivated, and well-meaning. He genuinely believed that

Church near Mexico City

95

the Mexican people wanted him as their Emperor; the cheering crowds, the floral archways, the flowers strewn at his feet, and the profound respect paid to him by high officers and dignitaries told him that he was beloved. He was not a nonentity; he would sometimes make speeches to the people in the towns he passed through, and they were good speeches. It pleased him that his beautiful wife was admired and adored, and he enjoyed the ceremonial life almost as much as he enjoyed the opportunity to issue imperial edicts, which were often liberal and sensible. What he did not know until it was too late was that he was merely the tool of the Church and the *hacendados*, and that Juárez, still riding across the country in his black carriage, possessed the affection of the people.

Within two years the new Mexican empire was crumbling all around Maximilian, and the liberals whom he attempted to conciliate would have nothing further to do with him. Carlota fled to Europe in the hope of receiving aid from Napoleon III and the Pope, but no aid came. With his small army under the command of the Indian general Tomás Mejía and the Mexican Miguel Miramón the Emperor fled to Querétaro. On May 15, 1867, Querétaro was betrayed, and the Emperor fell into the hands of his enemies.

Ever since he came to Mexico, he seemed to know he was doomed. There was a trial, which he refused to attend, but the issue was never in doubt. When someone brought him the false news that Carlota was dead, he felt only a great sense of relief that she would never learn about his execution.

Unknown to him, behind the scenes, powerful influences were at work to save him. Statesmen and kings were sending telegrams to Juárez, begging for a pardon or at least some remission of the death sentence: imprisonment perhaps, or a symbolic death, or perpetual banishment. Juárez read all these messages carefully, and said nothing. Even when Victor Hugo, the sworn enemy of Napoleon III, interceded in a voice of thunder, commanding Juárez to put aside all thoughts of revenge and to remember the sublime virtue of mercy, Juárez still said nothing. He was not concerned with anything so simple as revenge; what concerned him was justice. So he permitted the military court to make its own arrangements for the execution, which was set for June 16 at three o'clock in the afternoon.

At three o'clock that afternoon, having received the last sacraments, Maximilian stood at the door of his cell, waiting. No one came for him, and later in the day he learned that the execution had been postponed because the wife of

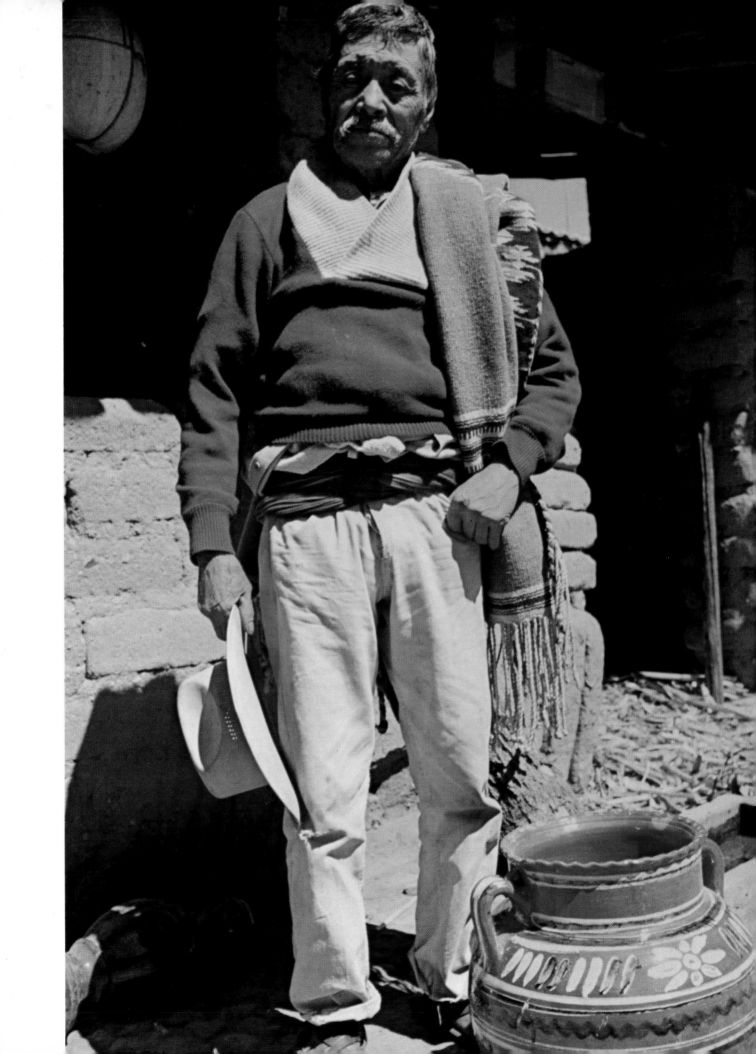

General Mejía was in childbed: the general would die, but he would be permitted to see his child before he was led out to execution with the Emperor. This was the single act of mercy which commended itself to Juárez, who recognized that a man has a right to see his own child, a right which was consecrated by natural law.

Early in the morning of June 19 Maximilian was awakened in his cell and for the second time, in the company of Miramón and Mejía, he uttered the prayer of contrition and received the last sacraments. He was dressed in full uniform, wearing a single decoration, the Order of the Golden Fleece, the golden lamb of sacrifice dangling at the end of a gold chain. At about six o'clock in the morning he was led down the stairway to the courtyard, where carriages were waiting. There were three carriages, one for each of the condemned men; and with a cavalry escort, the firing squad marching in the rear, the carriages lumbered through Querétaro, still dark with the early dawn. At the edge of the town Mejía's wife, with her newborn baby in her arms, suddenly flung herself out of a doorway. Screaming, she clutched the carriage which was taking her husband to his death. It was an easy matter for a guard to prick her hand with a bayonet and send her sprawling into the gutter. So the carriages lumbered on, while the church bells tolled and frightened eyes peered through the shutters. Soon they were in the open country, making their way to the Cerro de las Campanas, the hill where Maximilian had been captured, for it seemed only right that he should die in the place where he had seen the last vestiges of his power crumbling away.

At the foot of the hill the carriages came to a stop. The Emperor stepped out, and it was seen that his face was as white as paper and there was a cold sweat on his forehead. But he had more strength than his confessor, who would have fallen to the ground if Maximilian had not held him up. The small group walked up the hill toward a low adobe wall, part of the breastworks of the fortifications. A dense crowd watched in silence as the three men took up their positions beside the wall. At the foot of the hill four thousand troops were massed, to prevent any attempt to rescue them.

All the strange rites attending an execution were properly performed. Maximilian distributed gold coins to the firing squad, begging them not to aim at his face, and he thanked them for doing their duty. When the young captain in charge of the firing squad—he looked no more than a boy—asked his forgiveness, he gave it willingly. Miramón had indicated that he would like to have the place of honor

Fruit seller

101

in the center, and Maximilian granted him this final privilege. Seeing some people weeping in the crowd, he smiled at them, to indicate that they should have more courage. Then he looked down at the broad valley, the green copses, the small town shining in the early morning sunlight, and delivered his last speech, which was brief and carefully prepared: *"Muero por una causa justa,"* he said. "I die for a just cause. I forgive all, and pray that all will forgive me. May my blood flow for the good of this land. Viva Mexico!"

There was a volley. Three bullets tore into his chest, another into his forehead above the left eye. As he lay on the ground, face downward, he was heard to groan: *"Hombres! Hombres!"* The young captain rushed up and pointed with his sword at the Emperor's heart; an obliging soldier fired a fifth bullet which tore into the Emperor at such close range that his coat caught fire. He was the second Emperor of Mexico to die before a firing squad in less than fifty years.

The Emperor's death was remembered, and he became a legend, becoming more powerful in death than he had ever been in his life. His embalmed body was removed to Vienna and a plaster cast of his face, made some weeks after the execution, was solemnly preserved by the Mexican government, to be placed at last in a glass case in the museum at Chapultepec Castle. The embalmers had done their work badly; the face is in the last stages of disintegration. Like the Aztec statues, like the crucified Christs in the churches, he wears death royally. The terrible broken plaster cast, so imperious and so strong and so frail, thick with dust and falling to powder, is the closest thing in Mexico City to the dreadful Coatlícue, at once the mother of the gods and the Aztec image of death, in the museum.

But the legend of the youthful Maximilian remains, to haunt men's minds. He had done much in his brief reign to change the temper of his time. Austrian and French influences were to continue, and a certain graciousness, which he had fostered, was to be imposed on manners and styles. He enjoyed wearing Mexican clothes, he was passionately interested in archaeology, and he loved Mexico with the ardor of a convert. In design, in interior decoration, in architecture, in street planning, and in the cultivation of the arts he left an enduring imprint, so that Mexico City to this day resembles Vienna or Paris more than it resembles any city in Spain. The heavy ornamental Spanish style, black and gilded, gave place to one of lightness and grace, with all the colors of the rainbow.

It was not, of course, all his doing. General Bazaine and the French army of

occupation had much to do with it; the Frenchwomen who flocked to join their husbands or lovers did more. But Maximilian provided the focus and handed down the decrees. The Paseo de la Reforma, the most beautiful street in the Americas, came into existence at his bidding, and Chapultepec Castle was largely his creation. Long before it had become apparent to others, Maximilian recognized that the old Spanish quarter would eventually lose its importance. The old, moldering stones would crumble away, and a new city would spring up in the outskirts, just as the old medieval castles were eventually abandoned and towns sprang up at their feet.

No doubt for a few more years the Zócalo will remain the center of the city, but the flight from the center had already begun in Maximilian's time. Essentially it was a flight from Spain, from the overbearing insolence of the grandees and viceroys, the bishops and the tax gatherers, and the dark memory of the Inquisition. For too many years power had been concentrated in a small space thick with incense and imperial dignity. Everything spoke of authority: the sudden and merciless authority of Spain. Long after the revolution the capital remained Spanish. Then Maximilian came and shattered the mold. Now the city wanders across the whole valley, reaching out toward the surrounding hills, more splendid than ever because it has been given its freedom.

Balloons for a boy—
Sunday, Alameda Park

ZÓCALO

All Mexican history, they will tell you, flows through the Zócalo, and no doubt it did, but the times are changing. The guidebooks tell you that the great square was the site of the Aztec temples, and the guides will point out the exact spot where Moctezuma sat on his golden throne and watched the gashed and naked bodies falling down the immense stairways of the double temple, but guidebooks and guides are wrong, for no temples were ever built on the square. The square we see today was outside the temple enclosure, and the foundations of the great temples lie deep below the shopping area to the northeast.

Nevertheless that vast square, now so strangely empty and unadorned except for the buildings surrounding it, lies at the center of the mystery. Power radiates from it, as it did in the time of Cortés. It is not only that all the decrees are issued from the President's office in the National Palace, and that every year in September the Mexicans crowd into the square to hear the President summoning them to reaffirm their independence, and that the square itself is encrusted with legends, but in some strange and totally inexplicable way the Zócalo seems to have acquired a living presence and to be conscious of its historical role, in the same way that some ancient buildings acquire a presence on the edge of consciousness, or as a great bridge will give the impression of being conscious of its power to change men's lives, directing and channeling them according to its precise calculations. All things begin and all things end in the Zócalo, say the Mexicans; and there is only a white sheet of stone blazing in the hot sun.

It was not always, of course, a sheet of stone. The Zócalo has been many things and has served many purposes. It has a protean character and will assume whatever shape it pleases. It has been a park, a place for pageantry, a public execution ground, a bull ring, a camping site for revolutionary armies, a public market, a fairground, and, as we have seen, it once served as the private enclosure of a solitary statue.

Once for a brief time it really looked as though the Zócalo would become a permanent open-air theater. It happened not long after the arrival of the first viceroy, when a temporary truce had been declared between Cortés and the new

A friend

106

governor. The Emperor Charles V had patched up his interminable quarrel with the King of France by signing the Truce of Aigues Mortes in 1538, and when the news reached Mexico City there was a general desire to celebrate so auspicious an occasion. Cortés and the Viceroy vied with one another in magnificence and extravagance. The Zócalo was planted with trees, and many deer, foxes, jackals, and rabbits were let loose in the man-made forest, and in addition there were two young lions and four small tigers in cages. From the roofs of the surrounding palaces the spectators watched a forest battle of naked Indians armed with knotted cudgels. On the following day there was a pageant of Negroes all on horseback and adorned in gold and jewels from the treasure house of Moctezuma. On the third day the entire forest was uprooted, and instead there rose the fortress towers of Rhodes in painted wood with a canal cut through the square to represent the sea. The Knights of St. John had capitulated to the Turks in 1522 only a few months after Mexico capitulated to Cortés. In the confused scenario Cortés became the Grand Master Villiers de l'Isle Adam defending the fortress against Suleiman the Magnificent. Wearing his most ornate armor, he commanded the fleet that sailed across the square, no doubt remembering the days when he had sailed across the lake and put the Indians to flight. There was a good deal of mock jousting, the boom of cannon, and skirmishes by landing parties, with Indians and Turks and shepherds and bulls rushing helter-skelter across the fortifications, Cortés winning the battle, to the vast delight of the ladies of the conquistadors, who watched the pageant in safety, sipping their long cool drinks and stuffing themselves with marzipan and coated almonds. There was a comic interlude with Indians dressed up as Dominican friars plucking chickens or fishing from the ships. So Bernal Díaz describes the pageant at great length, remembering the color and excitement of mock battles as readily as he remembered real ones. Afterward there were two banquets, one given by Cortés, the other by the Viceroy, the meals being of gargantuan proportions and served on solid gold and silver dishes. Bernal Díaz, who had often gone hungry, records the menu to its last stupefying detail, adding that the Viceroy, a cautious man, took the precaution of seeing that his Indian servants kept watch over the gold plate in his possession; he lost only a few salt cellars, while Cortés, magnificently careless, took no precautions at all, and lost a fortune in silver, accounting it as nothing. "This," says Bernal Díaz, "was due to his *grandeza*, his grandeur."

From time to time there were more pageants on the Zócalo, but none of them ever equaled that first pageant in magnificence. As one colorless viceroy followed another, the life went out of the square, which became a market place, with the stalls being removed at intervals according to viceregal whims. The Count of Revillagigedo was the first to level it; Maximilian converted it into a public park. Then there was shade under the palm trees, and the fountains flowed, and once more the square possessed an appropriate beauty. It was not entirely an innovation, for there had been a small park fronting the Cathedral, and what Maximilian did was simply to extend the park across the whole length of the square. Maximilian's park survived until recently. In 1956 the trees were uprooted and the square was paved over, to become a parade ground and an arena for public gatherings. One day a new president will find new uses for the square, which seems so agonizingly empty.

Zócalo means "pedestal" in Spanish, and the name derives from the pedestal for a monument to Mexican independence set up in 1843. The pedestal waited so long for the monument that it became an object of affectionate derision. For seventy-seven years the pedestal remained there, and long before it was finally removed the whole plaza had become "*el zócalo.*" Under the Spaniards it was known as the Plaza Mayor, Plaza Principal, Plaza de Palacio, and Plaza de Armas. Under the Republic it became the Plaza of the Constitution. But this is the official term, to be used only by government officers and pedants who follow the lettering on official maps. For the Mexican people it is always the Zócalo, a word which rolls pleasantly off the tongue, to be uttered with an amused and ironical inflection.

What they remember, dimly perhaps, and perhaps only in the corner of the brain reserved for ancestral memory, is that the square saw the beginning of civilization in the New World. Here, or close by, the first fruits of Western civilization sprang from a robust tree. The first cathedral, the first hospital, the first school, the first university, the first printing press, the first library, the first mint, the first military barracks, and the first government office and tax bureau arose. Here, too, rose the first prison and the first gallows. The University was planned shortly after the Conquest and received its charter from Philip II in 1551, opening its doors as the Royal and Pontifical University of Mexico on January 25, 1553, the day of the Conversion of St. Paul, under whose protection it remained until Juárez instituted the reform laws abolishing the privileges of the Church.

Hawker working during bullfight

The house which saw the first sheet of printed paper in the New World still stands on the Calle de Moneda close to the mint which Maximilian converted into a museum, believing that Aztec sculptures deserved a better fate than to be left in the hands of university professors. The first hospital, dedicated to Jesus the Nazarene, was built by Cortés, who endowed it in perpetuity. It was built on the site where he first met Moctezuma robed in gold and jewels under a canopy of brilliant feathers. It was a memorable meeting and deserved a memorable monument; and it was characteristic of Cortés that he should choose a hospital as his only monument in the city. The hospital and its church were built in 1524, and near the altar his bones are buried.

The first fruits of civilization were often bitter, for priests and soldiers were the ruling power, neither being remarkable for their mercy. In Italy the newly discovered art of printing served to open the gates of learning and inquiry: in Spain the printer was the servant of the Church. The first printer in the New World was a Frenchman who went under the name of Juan de Pablo. He was summoned to Mexico City by Bishop Juan de Zumárraga to print books of Catholic doctrine in the Spanish and Indian tongues, and so it came about that the first book ever published in the Americas was a Spanish translation of *The Ladder to Paradise* by John Climacus, the sixth-century mystic and ascetic, who describes the vices that hinder a man from entering heaven and shows how, step by step, the vices may be overcome. No copy of the book has survived, but Pablo's other books, all heavily doctrinal, survive in a few rare copies. For fifty years, except for a book describing a volcanic eruption in Guatemala, all the books published in Mexico were concerned with Christian doctrine.

The Church stood at the apex of power, harsh and impenitent, currying favor with no one, not even with the viceroys in whom resided the ultimate power to shape the country's destiny. So the Church and the viceroy were often at odds, although outwardly they would attempt to show affection. The Cathedral stood close by the Viceroy's Palace, as the symbol of the enduring bond between Authority and Mystery. Cortés had chosen the site of the Cathedral, granting the Bishop only a few acres to build in. It would be a small church, covering only one half of one side of the square, unlike the Aztec temples that dominated the entire landscape. In the new city there would be an attempt to preserve the proper proportions; the cathedral would be subservient to the palace; on Sundays and

A novice with a bull

112

high holidays there would be stately processions across the square, and the bishop would welcome the royal governor at the gates, bless him, and escort him to his seat before the high altar. The intention was to build a cathedral that would be little more than a *cappella palatina*, the palace chapel of the governor.

The Cathedral grew slowly, painfully, with many fits and starts. Long after the new city had been built and fortified, the Cathedral was little more than a skeleton. Robert Tomson, an English traveler who reached Mexico City in 1556, a quarter of a century after the foundation stones were laid, says it was well built but half finished. It was, in fact, never completed, for Philip II was of the opinion that the existing Cathedral was disgracefully small and a far more sumptuous building was needed. He ordered the chief architect of his court, Alonso Pérez de Castañeda, to design a building that would dominate the entire square. The new Cathedral would be an edifice of colossal proportions, worthy of the power and majesty of the Church in New Spain. The blueprints were drawn up in 1667, and six years later the foundation stone was laid. There were the inevitable last-minute changes of plans, and there would continue to be sudden and abrupt changes during the entire course of the construction of the Cathedral, which lasted for a hundred and fifty years. Under twenty-four bishops, ten kings of Spain, and more than fifty viceroys, the work went on slowly—so slowly that men despaired of ever seeing it completed; and when, at last, in 1813, it was pronounced complete and perfect, the Church no longer possessed absolute power over the minds and souls of Mexicans, for the revolution that would eventually bring about the destruction of the special privileges of the Church had already begun.

This strange and gloomy Cathedral, the fruit of so many arguments and alterations, dominates the square by its sheer bulk, the heavy weight of dead stone. It seems to squat there like a beggar, driven by some inner compulsion to hunch its shoulders and bury its head between its knees, lost in dreams. The basalt and sandstone have not weathered well; there are days when it looks as though it had been carved out of lead, and by comparison the seven-hundred-and-fifty-foot façade of the National Palace is a model of grace and dexterity. The Cathedral is saved by the sacristy, which is altogether more graceful, giving the impression that it would leap into the air with joy if it were not held down by the weight of the Cathedral beside it. The sacristy, with its startling floral displays and wild growth of Churrigueresque decorations, sings, while the Cathedral groans.

Sunday painter, Chapultepec Park

The Mexicans themselves have little admiration for their Cathedral. In their eyes it is associated with the interminable years of bondage under Spanish rule, and they prefer to regard the basilica of the Virgin of Guadalupe as their national church. The basilica is light and airy; the Cathedral is dark and menacing. It might be at the bottom of the sea, encrusted with pearls and shellfish, festooned with decaying seafruit and adorned with the wreckage of ancient galleons. The weight of centuries lies upon it, and the chanting of the priests is drowned in darkness and immensity. Once you have entered it, there is the feeling that you will never escape, that you will sink deeper and deeper into the sea ooze and become one with the wreckage of the past. One dark chapel opens after another, one dark altar follows another, and there is no relief from darkness and despair. The heavy gilt ornaments have faded; the statues are flaking away; it smells of dampness and the tomb.

When Fanny Calderón de la Barca, the young Scottish wife of the Spanish Ambassador, came to Mexico City in 1839, she celebrated her safe arrival by attending Mass in the Cathedral. She was living near the Alameda Park; as they drove through the park, she was delighted with everything she saw. The fountains were sparkling in the sun, and the flowers were in full bloom. There were only a few carriages, and an occasional horseman could be seen through the trees. Beyond the park lay the Calle San Francisco, now Avenida Francisco Madero, and this, too, delighted her, for it was crowded with gaily dressed people going about their affairs. But when she entered the Cathedral, she was filled with horror. The floors were thick with dirt and dust, and there was scarcely anyone in the vast edifice except a sprinkling of *léperos* in tattered rags and blankets and some Indian women busily removing the nits from their hair. The priest was muttering to himself, his back turned to his congregation. She learned that women rarely attended Mass in the Cathedral, and the *léperos* were always on the watch for a handbag or a piece of jewelry, and there was more than a possibility of being physically assaulted by them. She had time to observe the splendid gold and silver vessels, and then heaved a sigh of relief and went out into the sunlight. A few minutes later she was contentedly examining the Aztec statues that were then housed in one of the cloisters of the University. The Aztec sculptures did not terrify her so much as the Cathedral.

Year by year the Cathedral sinks deeper into the oozy subsoil. Cracks appear

Sunday concert, Chapultepec Park

116

in the walls, the bell towers have a decided tilt, and one day the huge central dome may come crashing down on the worshipers. The wonder is that the Cathedral has survived so many earthquakes and so many architects.

For a few more years it will continue to dominate the Zócalo like the shadow of doom, and then it will vanish. In its place the Mexicans will build a cathedral of glass and steel, and the airy lightness of the Zócalo will be reflected in the mirrored walls, or perhaps—and this is more likely—there will be no cathedral at all, and the Zócalo will benefit by the added space. There are architects who speak of abandoning the old city altogether, for it is falling into the lake at the rate of a foot a year and there must come a time when the rate of subsidence will increase. They speak ominously of the day when the entire old city will vanish beneath the waters of the lake, when nothing will be left of the palaces of the conquistadors and the churches of the viceroys, and when people will go out in boats and look down through the blue waters at the lost city, which was once the most beautiful and splendid city of the Americas.

Sunday, Chapultepec Park—
Indians visiting Mexico City

THE MUSEUM
WITHOUT WALLS

In the twenties and thirties of this century the Mexicans began to turn with a sense of urgency to their Aztec past. The revolutions were coming to an end; the years of improvisation were over. For three centuries they had been ruled by viceroys, and only a handful of them had ruled well. With the single exception of Benito Juárez none of the presidents who ruled during the nineteenth century had brought any credit to the country. Two emperors had been shot by firing squads, and countless guerrilla chieftains had met a similar end. The country was poor, underdeveloped, and in need of peace, for the Indians, the mestizos, and those who still preserved their Spanish bloodlines were at each others' throats. There was a deepening sense of futility; it was as though they were destined to repeat in middle age the interminable adventures of their misspent youth. A Zapata or a Villa would arise, take possession of Mexico City, kill as many people as he could, and then suffer the inevitable betrayal. It was a country that appeared to have no culture of its own, at the mercy of forces beyond control, with little pride in its accomplishments and little hope of the future. Then in the course of a few years there occurred a renaissance. Mexico came of age. In the art of painting, in poetry, in architecture, and in the sciences the Mexicans began to discover themselves.

It was a strange and sudden awakening, for there had been little warning that it would ever come to pass. In its most obvious form the renaissance could be observed in the paintings of Rivera, Orozco, Siqueiros, and Tomayo, those "four horsemen of the Apocalypse," riding roughshod over all the acceptable academic codes and proclaiming that there existed an art that was wholly Mexican, independent of Europe. They painted with ferocious abandonment, in slashing colors, in a style (for they had much in common, even when they insisted that they were all enemies of one another) derived ultimately from their studies of pre-Columbian art. In the vigor of those ancient pottery figurines, in the majesty of the great Aztec statues, and in the brilliant coloring of Indian wall paintings they found

"The Bathers," Chapultepec Park

121

the impetus to create their own art. At the same time poets and architects were rediscovering the Indian past. They were haunted by Tenochtitlán and by the superb shapes of the pyramids of Teotihuacán and by the Aztec poems that had escaped the bonfires of the conquistadors. Their art was born out of a new respect for the past.

Both Tomayo and Rivera became collectors. They were not ordinary collectors; they collected on a massive and breath-taking scale. For his collection Rivera built a great moated Aztec palace, complete with ball park, on the outskirts of Mexico City. The palace no more resembled a real Aztec palace than Victorian Gothic resembles the Gothic of the thirteenth century. It was an improvisation on an Aztec theme, a palace such as Rivera might have lived in if he had been an Aztec prince. Tomayo, born in Oaxaca, is reserving his collection for his native city.

With the rediscovery of the Aztecs and of pre-Columbian art there came a reappraisal of the Spanish invasion. Rivera, basing his opinions on the work of the archaeologist Dr. Eulalia Guzmán, concluded that Cortés was a short, cross-eyed hunchback with a microcephalous skull and the general appearance of a monkey. Accordingly, when he painted his murals in the National Palace, he took pains to depict Cortés as a slight figure who looks as though he has recently escaped from a lunatic asylum. Dr. Guzmán later discovered the bones of Cuauhtémoc reposing in a secret grave in the village of Ixcateopan, together with a bronze plaque certifying that these were indeed the bones of the last Emperor of the Aztecs. Later it was learned that the bones included a female cranium and various odds and ends gathered from a charnel house. Nevertheless Rivera announced that it was the patriotic duty of all Mexicans to believe that the bones of Cuauhtémoc had been found. But these were merely the growing pains of the new age. The Mexicans had found their essential link with the past. The shapes and colors of pre-Columbian art provided them with a new source of energy, even a new way of looking at the world. The bones of Cuauhtémoc were no more authentic than Rivera's portrait of Cortés as a hunchbacked cretin, but the fact that people wanted to believe in them said much about the changing nature of the times. It is unthinkable that in 1900 anyone would have been deeply moved by the discovery of Cuauhtémoc's bones.

To house the national collection of ancient Mexican art the government has built a museum of quite extraordinary beauty. The building possesses a superb arrogance while remaining humble before the objects it displays. Calmly and purposefully it offers the appropriate setting for magnificence.

The weary visitor to the Louvre, the British Museum, or the Metropolitan Museum in New York enters a vast echoing hall discreetly empty of works of art, cavernous as a railroad station, with the best space given over to the selling of postcards. There is a clutter of small chaotic rooms, a sense of grim purposefulness. Directors, architects, and builders conspire with one another to discover the worst possible way to display works of art.

In the National Museum in Mexico City there are no cavernous halls for selling postcards. The architects designed a museum as it should be designed, giving the objects space and light and air to breathe in, and the visitor is offered all the temptations of a leisurely progress. A long, low, two storied house was built around a central patio, and set in a park among lakes and fountains. The house was modeled on the palace of Moctezuma, as described by the conquistadors, with wooden beams and bright tapestries and roof gardens, the rooms of a good size, and there were so many of them that one could easily lose oneself. What the Spaniards chiefly remembered of Moctezuma's palace was its essential simplicity and cleanness, the elegance arising from the very lack of the ornamentation they had expected.

So, here, in the museum, everything is simple, quiet, superbly functional. Occasionally you come upon floors of polished black marble, but mostly the floors are of inlaid wood, springy and sweet-scented. The roof beams are of mahogany and Mexican cedar, the walls are of glass, and the outside world comes flooding in. In the vast patio there is the inevitable pool, and at the very entrance to the patio there is a fountain. It is no ordinary fountain, for the water falls in a great ring around an immense carved stone pillar. The water thunders down, striking hard against a pavement of volcanic stone, so that for a moment you have the feeling that you have stumbled unaccountably upon a rain forest. The ring of falling water is a tribute to the rain god Tlaloc, lord of thunder and lightning and of all plants and flowers.

Tlaloc, indeed, is the presiding genius of the museum, being the most charming of the Aztec gods, with his crown of heron feathers, yellow hair, black face, and enormous gaping white eyes, through which the rain flows. The people of Mexico City have reason to remember his powers. In August, 1964, a few days before the

"The Revolutionaries," mural
by Juan O'Gorman in Chapultepec Castle

124

museum was officially opened, a much-weathered statue of the god was brought to the museum from an excavation site in La Venta. The statue weighed eighty tons and was borne on a giant truck with twenty wheels. It was a ten-hour journey, and people lined the streets to watch the progress of the god, taunting him for bringing them no rain. However, no one was particularly surprised when the greatest cloud-burst of the season took place the moment he arrived at his destination.

So, when you enter the museum, there is the thunder of falling waters to remind you of his presence, but as you move away the sound quickly diminishes until at last it becomes only a pleasant drumming noise heard faintly in the distance. Above the bronze column and the ring of water there is a vast textured alumimum canopy flashing silver in the sunlight.

Tlaloc, the silver canopy, the falling waters—all these are merely the intro-ductory flourishes to the unfolding spectacle. They surprise and enchant, because it is proper that there should be some surprising and enchanting object at the entrance of a museum. Beyond them lies Moctezuma's palace filled with treasure, with two great wings containing the regional arts of Mexico and the great sculp-tures and carvings of the Aztecs occupying the place of honor at the far end of the patio. Here and there the simple scheme has been broken by the addition of some unexpected treasure just outside the palace. You go down some dark steps into the eerie underground tomb of a prince whose bones and jade mask were found at Palenque, or you step out into a full-scale reproduction of the painted temple of Bonampak, or you find yourself contemplating a delicate white temple from Yucatan. Everywhere the objects are arranged so casually and intelligently that they seem to have found their proper place of their own accord.

Much art has been put into the setting and lighting, but it is an art that conceals itself. I have never known a museum where it is so easy to forget you are in a museum. No armed guards patrol the rooms, and there is never the slightest feeling that you have been permitted to enter on sufferance.

The museum officials are inclined to speak learnedly of the National Museum of Anthropology and History, as though it had some special scientific purpose. But this is merely a polite fiction. They know very well that the museum is a treasure chest. On the second floor there is an interminable ethnographical exhibition; we learn how the Indians reaped their corn, and what they wore, and what musical instruments delighted them, and no doubt this pleases the ethnographists. I suspect

Mexican wares in front of a mural
by Miguel Covarrubias

that when enough new treasures have been discovered, the ethnographic exhibition will be consigned to oblivion, together with the room devoted to the apotheosis of Juárez. The treasures are on the floor below, obstinately proclaiming their independence of science and their dependence upon great artists.

Pre-Columbian art can shake a man out of his mind and send him reeling after absolutes. It makes the art of many other civilizations look like decoration. Once you have grown accustomed to that powerfully convoluted line, the frets and the whorls, the flaring headdresses, the endless processions in light relief, those stern and nearly abstract countenances of serpents and jaguars, then pre-Columbian art is seen to possess an extraordinary vigor and authority. Even when they are being playful, those artists are triumphantly expressing divinity. They were concerned to depict the world of the gods, those stark and elemental presences who ruled their lives, and so they tore away all that separated them from the gods and saw them face to face. When they depicted Quetzalcóatl, the feathered serpent, they showed him in majesty, armored with feathers, with fierce eyes and curling fangs, so much larger than life that his head alone may be the size of a man. Or when they depicted Coatlícue, the mother of the gods, they depicted a squat figure who is almost an abstraction of power, made up of serpents and skulls and hands, and after you have seen her, it is unthinkable that the mother of the gods could be expressed in any other way. There is nothing warm or consoling about her. She does not invite caresses and she is wholly absorbed in her own affairs: imperturbable and final. She is death, and out of her womb there flows an abundant life. In these strange adventures with the gods the Aztec artists seem sometimes to be in collusion with divinity, possessing a knowledge we dare not possess.

If, for example, we set the towering figure of Coatlícue beside the Hermes of Praxiteles, we might find ourselves being puzzled at the thought that we once considered the Hermes to be a work of art. The Hermes says nothing that is not immediately apparent on the surface. Coatlícue says things about life and death that cannot be said in any other way. In some mysterious way the artist has succeeded in rendering her elemental force in stone. These artists strike hard before the vision fades, and all their carvings in stone have the ring of metal.

It is a world which is so foreign to us that it is necessary to enter it gradually, step by step, without impatience. We must accustom ourselves to a different line, a different conception of space, a different way of looking at the world. The Aztecs

Fresh, hot *tortillas*

were much closer to the earth than we shall ever be, and heard voices we shall never hear.

What concerned them ultimately was not so much the power of the gods—though their power could be felt and was manifestly visible in the heavens—as the presence of the gods in their daily lives. In a carving, in a painting, in a small figurine representing a jaguar, they could convey the immediacy of a divine presence. The green jade mosaic mask of a prince found beneath the lowest level of a temple in Palenque is evidently not a portrait. It is not intended that we should recognize the physical features. What the artist has given us is an expression of the essential dignity of the prince as he communes with the gods. It has an exquisite nobility, but it is not the nobility of the living. Out of a hundred pieces of jade and two sea shells the artist has constructed the portrait of a man who talks to the gods as their equal.

Again and again, coming round some corner of the museum, the power and beauty of ancient Mexican art startle you when you least expect to be startled. A clay dancer from Teotihuacán, two inches high, possesses a monumental elegance. The smiling goddesses from Vera Cruz are as haunting as the smiling goddesses of Greece. You become familiar with the feathered serpents and the permanently grinning jaguars; the skulls carved out of crystal or inlaid with jade no longer terrify; and even Coatlícue becomes a friend. At last the strange world of the Aztecs loses its strangeness, and you realize why the Mexicans have so great an affection for their past.

Detail of altar in
Church of San Francisco Javier, Tepotzotlán

THE DARK VIRGIN

Very early in the morning of December 9, 1531, a fifty-seven-year-old Aztec Indian called Cuauhtlatoahuac, which means "Singing Eagle," climbed up a low rocky hill at Tepeyac a few miles north of Mexico City and set in motion a strange series of events that profoundly altered the course of Mexican history. The stories and legends told about that early morning climb would be remembered by millions upon millions of Mexicans for centuries to come. Exactly what happened may never be known; what appeared to happen is known to nearly every living Mexican as though it happened to someone very close to him.

Cuauhtlatoahuac had been among the first Indians to be baptized, and he had been given the name of Juan Diego. His wife had died two years before, and he was living alone in the village of Tolpetlac, which, like Tepeyac, stood on the shores of Lake Texcoco. At Tepeyac there had been an Aztec temple dedicated to Tonantzin, goddess of the earth and corn, but this had been torn down after the Conquest and there remained only the rubble of the temple on top of the hill. In none of the surviving accounts, all written many years later, are we told anything of importance about Cuauhtlatoahuac. We learn that he owned a little property, that he had an uncle who received the baptismal name of Juan Bernardino, and that on that December morning he was on his way to Tlatelolco to attend a Mass in honor of the Virgin.

As he was walking at the foot of the hill he heard a voice summoning him in his own tongue, saying: "*Nopiltzin Juan, campa tiauh?*" ("Son Juan, where are you going?") He answered that he was on his way to Mass, and then he saw that the whole of the barren, rubble-strewn hill was shining with a strange light. He heard birdsong, but there were no birds. Following the voice, he climbed to the top of the hill. In front of him stood the Virgin, appareled in a garment of light, and she began to speak to him earnestly and simply, always in his own tongue. "Know for certain, littlest of my sons, that I am the perfect and perpetual Virgin Mary," she said, and went on to declare that it was her intense desire that her sanctuary should be built upon this rock. "Here I will demonstrate and show

myself, here I will offer all my love, my pity, my aid, and my protection to the people. I am the merciful Mother of all who live united in this land, and of all mankind, and all those who love me, cry to me, and seek me." Finally she commanded him to tell the Bishop to build her sanctuary on the hill of Tepeyac. "My son, you have heard my wish. Go in peace."

Bishop Juan de Zumárraga appears to have been annoyed because the Virgin addressed the Indian as "my son" and in addition he thought it highly unlikely that she would appear to an old Indian peasant. He sent the Indian away empty-handed. So, late in the afternoon Juan Diego returned to the hill of Tepeyac, to find the Virgin waiting for him. Falling on his knees, he explained that the Bishop had refused to listen to his plea, and that he would be more likely to pay attention if she sent someone of high and noble rank. The Virgin, possessing infinite patience and well aware of the frailties of bishops, commanded him to return to the Bishop's palace the following day and repeat the request. Accordingly, Juan Diego made a second visit to the Bishop, saying that the Virgin had appeared to him a second time and was waiting for an answer. The Bishop replied that if the Virgin really wanted him to exert himself, she should at least have the courtesy to send a sign, something that clearly belonged to her; otherwise he proposed to do nothing about her request.

In some confusion Juan Diego returned to Tepeyac, conscious that his mission had been fruitless and was likely to remain fruitless. The Virgin was waiting for him, and she promised to give him the sign the next day. It was dusk, the sun was setting, and soon she vanished. Juan Diego made his way home in the dark, only to learn that his uncle Juan Bernardino had fallen mortally ill. He spent the night by the old man's bedside and at the first dawn he was on his way to Tlaltelolco to summon a priest to administer the last sacraments.

According to the chroniclers, Juan Diego was in such a hurry to find the priest that he deliberately avoided taking his usual path beside the hill of Tepeyac and instead took the path by the lake shore, hoping to avoid the Virgin, who would only detain him when he had more important things to do. But from the top of Tepeyac she had watched his coming, and now she advanced down the hillside. Juan Diego begged to be allowed to go to Tlatelolco; he had a very important mission, and he would, he said, deal with her affairs later. Then, always speaking in the native tongue, she said: "Let nothing alter your heart or your countenance.

Tea in a turn-of-the-century hotel

134

Am I not your Mother? Are you not under my shadow and protection? Are you not in the crossing of my arms?"

Then she bade him climb with her to the top of the hill, for she now intended to give him the sign. Previously there had only been rocks and stunted cactus on top of the hill; now there was a field of Castilian roses in full bloom, and the air was filled with their perfume. She ordered him to pluck them and hand them to her. She arranged them, and then laid them in his cloak, the heavy cloak made of maguey fibers, which can be worn as a traveling bag, for many things can be hidden in the folds. As she tied the ends of the cloak in a knot at the back of his neck, she said: "This is the sign, which you are to give to the Lord Bishop. You are my ambassador, worthy of confidence. Do not let anyone see what you are carrying, and do not unfold the cloak until you are in his presence."

Juan Diego hurried off once more to see the Bishop. Inevitably, he was kept waiting, but the priests passing in and out of the antechamber saw how impatient he was and finally hurried him into the throne room. When Juan Diego opened the cloak to give the roses to the Bishop, there was a painting of the Virgin on the white maguey fibers. Fourteen days later a small chapel was built on the hill of Tepeyac and the first Mass was said before the miraculous painting. Some years later a basilica was built at the foot of the hill, and the painting was placed in it.

In the painting the Virgin, wearing a rose-colored tunic under her blue robe, stands on a dark crescent moon while golden sunrays pour out of her. Her head is bent a little to one side, her eyes are half closed, her hands are folded on her breast, and she stands in the familiar attitude of prayer. But what is chiefly remarkable about her is that she is dark-skinned, though there is a faint reddish glow like the reflection of a flame on her cheeks. She is *la Morena*, the dark one, the Virgin of the Indians, saying: "Are you not under my shadow and protection? Are you not in the crossing of my arms?" There is about her an air of humility and peace, of grave quietness and composure. The rose-colored tunic is heavily embroidered with a pattern of roses, and the blue robe has been dusted with stars. She stands there in a triple frame of gold, silver, and bronze, high above the altar, lit by batteries of lamps and by yard-long candles in immense silver candlesticks. The basilica has been built around her, and every perspective leads to her. Among those

Resting—Alameda Park

dazzling lights, amid all the gold and silver ornaments and marble statues, she reigns supreme. Priests move endlessly about, choirs sing, people are perpetually coming up from the nave and genuflecting before the image, there are continual processions of choirboys across the vast stage, and all this excitement and movement seem oddly out of place. Bells tinkle, the organ peals, the priests intone, and the storm of sound and color appears to be hurled against the painting, and to fall away. The Virgin is lost in her silence and never lifts her eyes.

Day after day, hour after hour, delegations come from all over Mexico to attend Masses at the shrine. In a single day there may be twenty Masses, and sometimes Masses are held simultaneously for different delegations. She is the Virgin of all Mexico, not only of the Indians; and the Cathedral in Mexico City has nothing to compare with her. So they come by train and in buses from all over Mexico, to ask her blessing and to venerate her. There is scarcely a house in Mexico that does not have her image. The cloak made of maguey fibers knits all Mexico together.

The Indians, of course, have a special affection for her, and they come in their hundreds and thousands. They make their way up to the altar rail on their knees, shuffling along slowly, murmuring prayers, their eyes fixed on the Virgin in the blue star-studded gown and the patterned rose-colored tunic. Those dark, handsome faces have a brooding eagerness, and in the middle of their prayers they will pause and talk to one another. A woman will open her dress and feed a child, and all the time she will be gazing at the Virgin. Awed children walk beside their shuffling, kneeling parents, like princes marching in the company of slaves. Although the prayers are spoken with urgency, there is nevertheless an air of gaiety. Children escape from their parents, skip, run, and hide under benches. They can make as much noise as they like, because all their shouting will be drowned by the organ. Hundreds of children have brought balloons to the shrine, with the result that the wooden ceiling is decorated with an astonishing number of captured balloons.

In Polish churches I have seen peasant women shuffling to the altar on their knees so painfully that the blood came. Here they shuffle slowly, without effort, without pain, as though they were delighted to kneel in the presence of the Virgin and saw nothing wrong in approaching her on their knees. They are continually talking to the Virgin, whispering, crossing themselves, smiling at one another,

The aristocracy

perfectly at ease. The shrine is their home, and they are inclined to regard the priests as interlopers who will inevitably demand a high fee to baptize a child or to say a Mass for the dead. So they avoid the priests, and go about their own affairs, and the most important of these affairs is to speak caressingly to the Virgin in their own language, pleading for her intervention, her mercy, her affection. They are not in the least concerned with the Church, but they are deeply concerned with the portrait she painted on Juan Diego's cloak.

Sometimes the Indians come with their arms full of flowers, leaving a trail of crushed petals on the stone floor, to the annoyance of the beadles, who are men of dignity and culture, with no particular fondness for the ill-dressed and slovenly Indians. The beadles are kept busy running after the Indian boys who jump on the benches in order to see better. The priests are far more interested in welcoming the official delegations, where everyone wears his best Sunday clothes and knows exactly when to genuflect. They are sleek priests, tending to fat, trained in Spain, and they betray a certain elegance. There is nothing in the least elegant about the Indians, who are alarmingly ill-equipped to take their places on the vast stage behind the altar rail. The priests worship in Latin, the Indians in Náhuatl. The two services go on simultaneously and independently. It is a satisfactory arrangement, and the Indians are perfectly content to let the Spanish priests use their church.

What is so pleasant about the basilica of *la Santísima Guadalupe* is that it is so light and airy, with none of the solemnity and gloom of the great Cathedral on the Zócalo. The gaily colored balloons, the striped rebozos, the flowers, and the children fill the place with color. There are no marble mausoleums of long-forgotten bishops, nor is there a *cora* to shield the priests from the faithful. All is open, radiant, flowering. The air comes rushing through the great gates and the doves coo in the beams overhead.

The Aztecs were always offering flowers to their gods, and so it is not surprising to find the modern Indians offering flowers to Christ and the Virgin, with great tenderness and affection. There is a life-size statue of Christ Crucified to the right of the altar, and as the Indians pass the statue they lift a flower to touch the feet of Christ and then cross themselves with the flower in a gesture of exquisite gentleness far removed from the perfunctory blessings of the priests. To touch with the flower, to make the sign of the cross, and then to hold the flower as though it had somehow

Fountain in Alameda Park

become even more precious—how delightful it is, and how much more genuine than the quick, ruthless gestures of the priests. The Indians perform these rites so naturally and meaningfully that one watches them with a feeling of awe, wondering how soon another miracle will take place. Faith burns in their eyes, but it is not the faith celebrated by the priests.

So they make their way, patiently and improvidently, throwing coins into every proffered coin box, until, having passed through some disreputable alleyways filled with shops selling religious trinkets and priests mechanically blessing for a fee of fifty centavos all the medals and rosaries held up to them, they come out at last to a stairway leading to the small church on top of the hill, built on the site where Juan Diego encountered the Virgin.

This should be, and perhaps once was, a church built with pride to honor a miraculous visitation. One expects to find a blaze of light and jewels, with a prodigious display of Mexican murals. It would be a treasure casket with all the most sumptuous offerings gathered in a little space, like the Cappella Palatina in Palermo, which is not very much larger than a drawing room but has the most perfect mosaics in Sicily. Alas, the hilltop shrine is a small, dark, narrow, rather sinister place with some gaudy nineteenth-century paintings depicting Juan Diego kneeling before an aristocratic, full-bosomed Virgin, who has obviously stepped off the cover of a chocolate box. The landscape is muddy, Juan Diego looks as though he has been set down in a photographer's studio and is thoroughly bored, and the angels wear sombreros. The Indians enter listlessly, and go out just as listlessly. They had expected a blaze of magnificence, a fountain of pure light, and there is only a small, dark, dusty anteroom, which appears to have no purpose whatsoever except perhaps to serve as a mortuary chapel for the cemetery behind it or as a tourist trap, for there are the usual shops selling rosaries, hot dogs, and *hamburguesas* close by.

There is however one object in the church that inspires fear amounting to pure terror. This is a Christ Crucified of black wood, the color of coals, standing in the small and narrow transept. He wears a purple velvet loin cloth and at first sight you would take it for just another crucified Christ like all the others which crowd the Mexican churches. But this one, so dark in the shadows, so dreadful in the gleaming blackness of the sunburned skin, has a special vehemence of agony. Blood pours from a wound in the head, from the eyes, from the mouth, along the beard, from a gaping wound in the chest, from the broken knees and the torn feet,

The Angel, guardian of Mexico,
on the Monument to Independence,
Paseo de la Reforma

142

and seems to come in a steady pulsing flow. Christ writhes in agony, and at any moment you expect him to lurch off the wall and come crashing down on the stone floor.

I have never seen another Christ like this, and do not expect to see another. The Mexican sculptors generally depict the agony with an intensity outreaching all the efforts of the Spanish sculptors, who concentrate the agony on the face. In Mexico the whole body of Christ is in violent agony, and the Mexicans remember, as the Spanish sometimes forget, that the knees were broken and the entire articulation of the legs suffered from the heavy blows across the knees. The Mexicans can make Christs out of straw and still suggest the agony by the way the head droops and the arms are flung apart, and they habitually make Christs in vivid colors. I have seen blue and yellow Christs, and one that was vermilion, and I have marveled at the Mexicans' terrible gift for suggesting the shapes of agony. But the black Christ of Tepeyac belongs to another order. The conventional agonies have been forgotten in this stark and visionary portrait, so living and so dead. The eyes glare, the hair is drenched with sweat, the open mouth sucks desperately at air, and the tormented body turns and twists in an agony of despair with a violence beyond anything known in other Crucifixions. I suspect it is a very old work, going back to the time of the conquistadors, made by an Indian convert to the faith who had pondered deeply on the mystery of Christ's death. It is a work to chill the blood. There, finally and triumphantly, in that abandoned corner of a small and insignificant chapel, the Mexican genius for rendering the agony of death achieves its perfect expression.

The black Christ moves us by the sheer terror he inspires, the dark Virgin by her gentleness and grace. What is strange about the black Christ is that he is totally unexpected—being in the wrong place, in a shrine sacred to the Virgin—and that it is a work of superb art. What is strange about the dark Virgin is that she is totally expected, and the image painted on the white cloak seems to be absolutely right and appropriate, though it is not a great work of art.

One finds oneself returning to contemplate it again and again, as though there were some mystery that could be penetrated simply by gazing at it. Many have observed that the painting is quite small; the Virgin is no more than four and a half feet tall, yet she seems to dominate the immense basilica. The colors have faded, the design is oddly static, and the angel who supports her robes was evi-

Fountain in Alameda Park

dently a later addition damaging the entire composition, but the total effect is enchanting.

There is some mystery about the true origin of the painting. Few people have been permitted to examine it closely, and no one has ever been permitted to remove the glass. Don Joaquín García Icazbalceta, a well-known nineteenth-century historian, was asked by the Archbishop to examine the available documentary evidence. As a Catholic layman and eminent scholar, he could not refuse the request, though he felt a certain reluctance; he knew the documents well enough to realize that they could offer no proof of a miracle and might even dispose him to believe that no miracle had taken place. In his private report to the Archbishop, published after his death without the authorization of the Church, he wrote that he had come regretfully to the conclusion that the painting was made by an Indian artist from the neighboring convent of Santiago Tla/telolco, where the Franciscans had founded an academy to train young Indian painters. Contemporary evidence of the miraculous portrait was lacking; there was nothing in the extensive writings of Bishop Zumárraga to suggest that he was aware of its existence, nor was there anything in the writings of the other prominent churchmen who were acquainted with him and discussed it with him. Don García Icazbalceta believed the story may have come about as the result of an innocent folk drama performed by the Indians. As they acted out the drama of Juan Diego's encounter with the Virgin in the presence of the painting, the painting itself became part of the drama. The real story of Juan Diego had perhaps ended with the shower of roses falling from his cloak.

What is certain is that the painting came into existence because the Indians wanted it and needed it. If Christianity were to become tolerable to the conquered people, then it became abundantly necessary that Christ or the Virgin should speak to them directly and perform for them a special act of charity. They knew death well enough—they had received it abundantly from the conquistadors—and what they needed was mercy and protection. "Are you not under my shadow and protection? Are you not in the crossing of my arms?"

The cult of the painted cloak grew slowly, and it was not until 1575 that a proper shrine was erected for her over the objections of the Franciscans, who pronounced that the painting was unworthy of veneration; the battle between the secular clergy and the monks had already begun. In 1629 Mexico City was inun-

A photographer in Alameda Park

dated and a large part of the city was destroyed. The Archbishop, Don Francisco Manzo, gave orders that the Virgin of Guadalupe should be brought to the city and placed in the Cathedral. The floods subsided, the Virgin returned to Tepeyac in triumph, and thereafter her image began to appear all over Mexico. But it was not until 1810, when the white-haired Father Miguel Hidalgo raised the banner of revolt in Dolores—his banner was a painting of the Virgin of Guadalupe—that she became the acknowledged patron of Mexico, the divine protectress of the nation. When independence came, then this, too, was seen to be her handiwork, her gift to her beloved Mexicans.

The basilica at Guadalupe became the most hallowed place in Mexico, and even at the height of anticlerical persecutions, when churches were being sacked and priests were being immolated, the basilica remained intact. Once a bomb was placed under the altar. It exploded, twisting a crucifix, but left the image of the Virgin unharmed. When Emiliano Zapata rode roughshod through Mexico at the head of his Legion of Death, capturing Mexico City three times, making and breaking presidents at will, he flew the banner of the Virgin of Guadalupe, and, being a brigand, very well aware of his mission, he added a black skull and cross-bones at her feet. He died a brigand's death, being cut down by a man he thought to be his friend, and his head was hung up outside the National Palace until it became as black as the skull he had painted on his banner.

Over Mexico the Virgin of Guadalupe reigns supreme. With half-closed eyes, her head inclined a little to one side, wearing delicate pastel-colored robes, she offers her peace to all the Juan Diegos of this world, at home in her enchanted palace, where the doves nest in the roof beams and the ceiling is festooned with colored balloons.

Rufino Tamayo, classic painter

WAXWORKS

One day when the sky was very high and glowing, I came out of the basilica of the Virgin of Guadalupe into the glare of the white plaza. Some Indians were dancing close to the basilica, wearing only loincloths and enormous rainbow-colored feathered headdresses, which quivered and swayed wildly as they danced, whirling like streams of butterflies. They were powerful men, bronzed and wonderfully agile, and they danced well, but the small crowd around them looked on dejectedly. They had seen Indians dancing so many times, and it was always the same dance. A few peasant women were making their way across the plaza on their knees, and sometimes they were accompanied by a boy who laid a piece of cloth on the pavings just in front of them, and in this way they would crawl over the cloth and so accomplish a few more inches of their journey. These Indian peasant women crawled with great dignity, though sometimes sweat, like tears, would form on their faces.

It was one of those days when a nearly empty square can inspire fear. The sky was a little too bright, the pavings a little too smooth, the sounds of the city too far away. Alone at midday, on any Mexican plaza, you have the feeling that you are entering a Chirico landscape where everything has been frozen in an interminable eternity and the clock ticks out the hours with the slow tolling of bells. How many years would pass away before the woman in the red serape, crawling on her knees, would reach the lowest step of the basilica? The bronzed Indians were still dancing, but the small crowd had drifted away. Here and there blue pigeons were sunning themselves. A priest hurried like a shadow across the plaza, and then vanished. It was, I reflected, one of those days when people slide through the white gates of the air and are never seen again. The glare of the plaza was blinding.

There was a time when all that plaza was crowded with hucksters' booths and playgrounds; Indians camped around the basilica; there was always noise and uproar. The basilica in those days was much smaller, and there were not so many gold ornaments, and the painting of the dark Virgin was lower, almost within reach. I confess I preferred it that way, for the present basilica resembles a vast theater in which there are perpetual performances.

Architect Felix Candela

I wandered along the Calzada de los Misterios in search of shade. A few steps down the road there was a waxworks show. A gramophone was blaring away; a fat redheaded woman beckoned pleasantly, demanded some money, and waved the curtains aside. Here, then, on this highway, beside the grocers' shops and the dressmakers, was the last relic of the fairground which had once greeted all visitors to the shrine of the Virgin of Guadalupe.

I expected nothing from the waxworks, for recently in Rome near the Church of Santa Maria Antiqua I had come upon a waxworks of such unencumbered tawdriness that it seemed impossible to believe that anything could be worse. The wax was crumbling away, the eyes were falling from their sockets, the wigs were askew, and the clothes were patched and moth-eaten. The place was damp and smelled of a latrine. At least, I reflected, these waxworks can be no worse than those of Rome.

Grateful for the shade, the darkness, the sense of security that comes from entering a small space after wandering blindly across an immense plaza, I was content to walk among the waxworks like a ghost at home among ghosts. These ghosts were familiar, for all waxworks must have them. There was, for example, the inevitable Charlie Chaplin, the cheeks too ruddy, the mustache too large, the tilt of the derby at the wrong angle. There was Pope Pius XII with a wax hand raised in blessing, the purple lips formed in such a smile as he never showed except perhaps at the moment of death. There was Emiliano Zapata, the ferocious revolutionary, looking slim and youthful, his thumbs tucked into his black waistband, his feet apart, in the attitude he assumed whenever he was being photographed. There was nothing in the least ferocious about him, for he looked like a shopwalker, and the huge mustaches were no more than decorative tributes to those ancient photographs. Decidedly, there was nothing to be gained by going any farther.

Upstairs there was Frankenstein, and I thought I detected a glimpse of the true wax molder's art in the portrait of Boris Karloff with a knife protruding from his back. There was life in it; the heavily lidded eyes concealed many mysteries, and he emerged out of the darkness with a proper malevolence. Evidently there were two wax molders, for the artist who made Frankenstein had nothing in common with the artist who merely took a model from a shopwindow, stuck two heavy mustaches on it, and called it Zapata. The Frankenstein artist had made a commendable portrait of James Dean, the rebel without a cause, who is in danger of

Diana fountain, Paseo de la Reforma

becoming a Mexican folk hero. The Zapata artist had contrived a great panorama of the Virgin of Guadalupe, which occupied a place of honor among tinsel flowers. There was no mystery about her; she, too, had been taken straight from a shop-window, and Juan Diego's imploring gaze was oddly unconvincing, perhaps because one eye was blue and the other green. Perennial visitors to waxworks know they will eventually reach a point of horror and disgust, and only the most hardened waxwork watchers stay beyond this point. The making of waxworks is a lost art, and there is little evidence that it will ever be revived.

Still, there was the Frankenstein artist to contend with. I went back to see his work, and was more than ever convinced of his mastery. Somewhere in Mexico there was an artist of quite extraordinary powers, capable of breathing life into wax. James Dean with his open shirt and cigarette dangling from his lips was the very image of the real James Dean. Frankenstein was truly and inescapably Frankenstein. If he could do these, surely he could do others; and so I went down the rickety staircase to see the remaining exhibits, with the feeling that there might be at least one more example of the work of the Frankenstein artist.

I had almost given up hope when I came to the last exhibit. Against a green curtain there stood a figure of grave authority and indisputable grace, with the breath of life in him. He was dark-faced, saturnine, with wide-open eyes which had not been simply inserted into the eye sockets but belonged there by right, like the deep furrows in the forehead and the mocking curl of the lips. Lank hair escaped from under his black broad-brimmed hat and drifted down to his shoul-ders. He looked ill, perhaps tubercular; he was pleading that we should buy his wares—those fine-toothed combs, shoelaces, laces, ribbons, stockings, and cotton thread—which he carried under his arms in wicker baskets. Bells hung from his hat and more bells hung from his baskets, and there were still more fastened to his coattails and his ample pockets. His clothes were ragged and patched, and their general color resembled dark green slime. The bells were of all sizes—little bells the size of thimbles and others as large as cowbells—and they gave the patched clothes an astonishing gaiety, while the cluster of bells on his hat had something of the appearance of a feather, a feather of gold, such as a nobleman might wear in medieval times. The combination of ragged clothes and shining bells gave him a vaguely aristocratic air, as of a man who knows how to decorate himself to proper effect although he has come down in the world. He leaned forward a little, and it was this which gave him the look of a man pleading, whereas if you examined

The dreamer

155

his expression more carefully, you saw that he was totally indifferent to everyone he encountered and lived in a dark secret world of his own.

It was not only that there was malevolence in him, but he seemed in some mysterious way to hate his own malevolence, perhaps because it was not directed at the world outside but at himself. He did not live for the things men live for, and he practiced vices which are little known. It was a world enclosed, very powerful, frightening in its intensity. Of course, all this did not emerge for some time. It was a figure to be examined closely, as one examines the Donatellos in the Bargello, looking at them from all sides, hoping to catch that precise angle that somehow reveals all the other angles. This beggar with the bells had a shocking power. He leered, he beckoned, he hinted at madness. The gramophone was playing "*La Cucaracha*," and this seemed somehow appropriate, for the melody has overtones of madness. And if not madness, then this strange figure with the dark, pointed nose and thick-veined hands hinted at a strangeness that was beyond any comprehension, for he did not belong to this world. I got down on my knees to see him better, stood at one side, played all those necessary tricks one plays with an authentic work of art, and he was all of a piece. It was the strangest thing to find in a waxworks—a work of monumental power.

All this the Frankenstein artist had accomplished with apparent ease. Out of wax he had carved the character of a whole man, alive and unforgettable, terrible in his malice, cynical, penniless, half down-at-heels nobleman, half foot-loose beggar. Out of those immense weary eyes there came sparks of pent-up fury. The artist had penetrated deep into his soul, letting nothing escape him.

This was, I reflected, something that had never happened before and was not likely to happen again. For a moment I wondered whether an actor had slipped into the place and amused himself by assuming the posture of a waxwork, for the lips appeared to form in a fleeting smile, the eyes appeared to dance maliciously, and certainly there was something of the actor in that strange troubling presence. I imagined one of those threadbare actors who wander in all seasons from village to village, jaded and corrupt, singing ballads and acting out his roles on a table set in the middle of the plaza, one lecherous eye fixed on the village maids while the other followed the movements of his associate, the pickpocket, his companion in misfortune. If he were an actor, this would perhaps explain the bells, but it would not explain the baskets full of knickknacks. So I came reluctantly to the

conclusion that he was nothing more than an itinerant peddler suffering from some ferocious spite against mankind.

There was a printed notice beside him. It read: PITO PÉREZ, but the name meant nothing to me. I went out into the glare of the Calzada de los Misterios haunted by the fire in the man's eyes and elated by the discovery that there existed a wax molder of genius. There were some shops selling jewelry, and it was pleasant to discover a necklace of hammered silver and imitation emeralds made by a master craftsman for a price I could afford. Decidedly, things were looking up. The Virgin of Guadalupe was scattering her blessings.

During the following days I remembered Pito Pérez with pleasure. Who was he? No one seemed to know, and it no longer seemed important to know where he came from; it was enough to rejoice in the memory of a gay and rather sinister scoundrel who was probably the hero of a half-forgotten nineteenth-century novel, one of those novels where the picaresque adventures of a wanderer are recounted at vast length. One day, at a party, a learned Spaniard told me the story of Pito Pérez. "He is the original Mexican folk hero," he said. "He has always been in Mexico, but he was born only thirty years ago in the mind of José Rubén Romero. In every Mexican you will find something of Pito Pérez." It appeared that Pito Pérez was not the invention of a nineteenth-century novelist, but of a distinguished Mexican diplomat and scholar, who wrote the novel in 1938 while serving as Mexican ambassador to Brazil.

La Vida Inútil de Pito Pérez is a very short novel, scarcely more than a long short story. We meet Pito first in a bell tower as he takes a last lingering look at his native village. With his bulky shoes, his ill-fitting celluloid collar and patched coat fastened with a safety pin, his trousers so baggy at the knees that he could have kept his children in them, his great mop of black hair with a wide-brimmed straw hat perched precariously on top, and a flower in his buttonhole, he derives from a recognizable source. He is Charlie Chaplin wandering foot-loose over Mexico. He tells the story of his life, and it must be admitted that the story has been told many times before. As an altar boy he stole from the poor box, and in the course of his misspent life he engaged in every kind of petty thievery. He was always wandering from one village to the next in search of an easy penny, rarely finding it. He once served behind the counter of a druggist's store and he had a merry time mixing prescriptions according to their colors, to the extreme danger of the villagers. He did not enjoy prison, but prisons seemed to have a great fasci-

Next two pages
The Zócalo, facing the National Palace,
built by Cortés on the site of
Moctezuma's palace

Right
El Caballito, "the little horse,"
with its rider, Charles IV

158

nation for him; he was always being arrested, and for shouting down the judge he would receive a longer term of imprisonment than he thought he deserved. He recounts his adventures with a certain dignity, but since they are the casual adventures of any picaresque hero, they are no better and no worse than many others.

Toward the end of the book, however, there is a sudden and dramatic change of tempo. Many years have passed, and a new Pito Pérez enters a wineshop to relate his further adventures to the author. He comes with his baskets filled with gewgaws, with bells in his hat and the light of madness in his eyes, stern, irascible, full of hatred for the human race. He has seen the revolutionary wars and made his peace with women, with death, with all the useless ceremonies of living. From an anatomical laboratory he has stolen the bones of a woman which accompany him wherever he goes. Death is his bride, and it pleases him to be photographed with his bride, who has no bodily functions, no body odor, and demands nothing in the way of clothes and jewelry. She is not in the least capricious, and she is the model of all virtue. "Look at her big eyes, her white teeth, and notice that over her heart she wears a sprig of orange blossoms like the one I wear pinned on the lapel of my jacket," he roars, displaying the photograph of the newly married couple. "The Epistle of St. Paul says that marriage ends only in death. Mine begins with death and will last throughout all eternity."

So he rages deliriously, describing the virtues of his bride, the horrors of living flesh, the blessedness of bones. There is a hardness in him, a corrosive bitterness, and he is not quite so mad as he seems, for against every argument in favor of life he has a better argument in favor of death. There is something in him of the early Church Fathers, for he is an impenitent devotee of the joys of heaven as distinguished from the joys of earth. Gaunt, drunk, hopelessly at odds with the world, he chants a dirge over the incorrigible frailties of mankind, and spits in the world's face. At such moments he possesses a kind of elemental grandeur. He is no longer an amiable purse thief; he has become Lucifer.

Nothing in the early part of the novel has prepared us for those powerful last pages where Pito Pérez denounces the world and all its trumperies. They were evidently written at white heat, and it is these pages the Mexicans remember gratefully, not because the cause of Lucifer is expressed with so much venom and relish, but because Pito Pérez displays a fierce dignity and humanity even when he is

Students of the National Preparatory
School No. 1 in front of mural by
José Clemente Orozco

assailing humanity. A few days later he is found lying dead on a rubbish heap. In his pocket there are a few lines scribbled in pencil:

LAST WILL AND TESTAMENT

To Humanity, I bequeath the entire lot of my bitterness.

To the rich, hungry for gold, I leave the excrement of my life.

To the poor, because they are so cowardly, I will my contempt—because they do not rise and seize everything in one final stroke of supreme justice. Miserable slaves of a church which preaches resignation to them; miserable slaves of a government which asks complete submission without giving them anything in return!

I believed in no one! I respected no one! Why? Because no one believed in me, because no one respected me. Only fools or lovers give themselves without some conditions.

LIBERTY, EQUALITY, FRATERNITY!

What a ridiculous farce! Liberty is murdered by those who have power. Equality is destroyed by money. And Fraternity dies at the hands of our own miserable egoism.

Humanity, I stole some money from you; I made fun of you; my vices ridiculed you. I do not repent! And at the very moment of my death, I wish I had the strength to spit all of my scorn into your face.

I was a drunkard. A nobody! A walking truth. What madness! And there, walking on the other side of the road, Honesty displayed her decorum and Wisdom showed off her prudence. The struggle has been unequal, and this I understand. But out of the mettle of the humble there will surge one day an earthquake and then no stone will remain upon another.

Humanity, I shall soon collect what you owe me!

Such was the last will and testament of Pito Pérez, who wore a cap of bells and sold laces to village women, as written by the eminently respectable Don José Rubén Romero, former university professor and twice ambassador. You can see Pito Pérez walking down any street of Mexico, but you can see him to best advantage in the waxworks on the Calzada de los Misterios, across the square from the basilica of the Virgin of Guadalupe.

Santísima Muerte, detail from "A Dream of a Sunday Afternoon in the Central Alameda Park," mural by Diego Rivera in the Hotel del Prado

SANTÍSIMA MUERTE

All over Mexico there can be found representations of another goddess at least as powerful as the dark Virgin of Guadalupe. This goddess rules as sovereign over a vast and increasing empire, and though she offers gifts and wears an immaculate finery, the face that peers through the embroidered headdress is never pleasant to look upon. Her gifts are poisonous, her face is a skull. She is not a virgin, and if she resembles anyone at all, it is an old hag from a child's fairy tale. She is *Santísima Muerte*, most sacred Death, and her power reaches over the living and the dead.

Like other saints she has her name day, her particular forms of worship, her liturgies, and her special prayers. Since she is peculiarly Mexican, and the Catholic Church is inclined to frown on her and even to suggest that she has no existence, she belongs among the category of saints who have no known abode, although it is generally accepted that she rules over a corner of heaven. The dying pray that at their last moments they may be elevated into the presence of her divine majesty, and they will sometimes speak of her as *"Santísima Muerte querida de mi corazón"* —"most sacred Death, beloved of my heart." It is proper to placate her, to speak of her yearningly and tenderly, and to hope that she will prove to be ultimately beneficent. Yet she is not one of those saints with whom men can live on intimate terms. She holds herself at a distance—remote, implacable, and strangely silent.

She is usually represented as a skeleton clothed in a long white priestly gown with ample sleeves, and she carries herself with a certain priestly elegance. In her right hand she holds the scales of justice and in her left hand, the orb of the universe; although no one has ever doubted that she has power over the universe, it is difficult to understand why she should bother with the scales of justice. One imagines that justice is very far from her thoughts, and, indeed, she is scarcely concerned with justice at all. What interests her to the exclusion of nearly everything else are her power and her undying permanence.

She wears a widow's cowl, with two long lappets stretching down over her thin breasts, and her white gown swirls around her, so that she appears to be advancing. Her head is bent a little to one side, as she smiles invitingly. She has a

The thieves' market on a Sunday

certain nobility; and though one might mistake her for a ghost or a bag of bones emerging from a long-concealed closet, on a second glance there is no doubting that she descends from imperious ancestors. *Santísima Muerte* is no parvenu. She has been on the earth, the Mexican earth, for a very long time.

She descends, of course, from the ancient Aztec gods, and chiefly from the goddess Coatlícue, the mother of the gods, whose face is two serpent heads, whose skirts are writhing serpents, and whose necklaces are formed of human skulls, hands, and hearts. In the Museum of Anthropology the goddess Coatlícue stands more than eight feet high, and possesses a ferocious grandeur. The Aztecs knew how to suggest her mysterious and unfathomable powers. They knew her well, for they had entered her kingdom and seen her with their own eyes. In that vast block of stone, heavy with the weight of mortality, once richly colored and now an undifferentiated gray, there is the image of a power beyond all power, a passion beyond all passion. Those cold and unquestioning serpents' eyes, those human adornments, and the heavy broken surface suggest authority in its ultimate aspect; she is magnificent in her ruthlessness and her indifference to the pleas of mankind. There, at last, a great sculptor depicted something which one would have thought beyond the power of any sculptor—the absolute majesty of death.

Santísima Muerte is merely the down-at-heels descendant of a far greater goddess, the last poor sprig of a long line. She is no more fearsome than any skeleton dressed up in a sheet. Her Spanish elegance is her undoing, and though she may frighten children, she cannot frighten grown men. As she is usually portrayed, modeled in brilliantly colored sugar candy, or in plaster statues, or in engravings and worn, fingered postcards sold at the church gates, there is always something mincing in her walk, in the swirl of her gown. She smiles and tilts her head too invitingly for anyone to believe in her promise of eternal bliss.

The Mexicans adore her; she is, after all, someone they know very well. If she no longer wears the august authority of Coatlícue, she remains a familiar presence. Death rides wild in Mexico, where whole villages die of starvation and killing is not regarded as one of the seven deadly sins. Tempers flare; a gun is pulled out; *Santísima Muerte* steps in to claim her casual victory. She is present wherever men congregate, so that it is sometimes a relief to escape to the wild hills. At the end of the nine-day Christmas holiday the police in Mexico City count up the dead; there were one hundred and two in 1967, and no doubt there will be more next year. Sooner or later the Mexican authorities will be confronted with the task of making it difficult for anyone to own a revolver.

Plaza of the Three Cultures:
Aztec temple, colonial church,
and modern housing development

169

So Death rides high and wild, and there is no escape from her, and *Santísima Muerte*, descending from her pedestal, becomes the painted candy skull, to be licked and eaten by children, who have scarcely any need to be reminded of her presence. The skulls are heaped up in the market place, like apples. They come in all colors and sizes. There are pink skulls, green skulls, yellow skulls; most of them have empty eye sockets, but sometimes the sockets are filled with sugar almonds. There are fleshy skulls, and skulls so thin and woebegone that they cry out for a larger coating of sugar. There are skulls with painted lips, and others with false eyelashes and yellow wigs. There are even skulls with pearly encrustations of necklaces and earrings, though there are no ears. The Mexican confectioner has excelled himself in producing such a gay diversity of skulls that one wonders, as one wonders about women's dresses, how anything so simple could be so infinitely variable. Some skulls are laughing, some crying, some pouting, some daintily preening themselves. The skulls for the very rich are fashioned with all the refinements of the jeweler's art, like Fabergé eggs, and no doubt there is some remote connection between the faceless eggs of imperial Russia and the egglike skulls of Mexico City.

In Sanborn's, the blue-tiled drugstore on Avenida Francisco Madero, I once watched an old aristocratic woman, regal in purple, wearing a purple veil, as she fingered a tray of skulls with remarkable deftness. The skulls at Sanborn's are fashioned for the *haut monde*, painted in delicate pastel shades, with curly hair and looking very feminine, and there are even skeletons dressed up in frilly clothes and wearing painted slippers. The old woman spent a long time fingering them, as though determined to find one of exactly the right consistency, rejecting now one and now another, murmuring to herself as she pored over them until the shopgirl was almost out of her mind. At last, with an expression of exquisite weariness, as of someone who has accomplished a purpose which has long been maturing in her mind, she chose a skull resembling a doll, with red spots on the cheeks, a wig of manicured ringlets, and eyelashes an inch long. Appropriately, the skull was placed in a little white box, which was tied with a blue ribbon. No doubt the old lady had found a suitable present for her youngest granddaughter.

You see the skulls everywhere, in every shop, in every market place, in every street. An automobile flashes past, and there is a skull speared on the radio antenna. A small boy is walking down a street, calmly and intently sucking a lollipop, but it is not an ordinary lollipop. What he is sucking is a sugar-candy skull with his

Devotees and penitents at Guadalupe shrine

own name written boldly across the forehead. Jewelers make skulls out of gold. There are days when every department store seems to have paper skeletons swinging in all the windows, suspended on springs and in perpetual gyrating motion. There are even skulls made of neon lights, winking in blue and crimson. Every resource of human ingenuity has been brought into play to celebrate the victories of *Santísima Muerte*.

Why this infatuation with death? Defiance? Despair? Delight? Ancestral memory? The Mexicans themselves discuss their infatuation at length, and very calmly, for they regard death imperturbably. Their minds feed on inconsistencies, and for them death is the ultimate inconsistency, the supreme irony. The intellectuals write learnedly about the idea of death, in terms of categories and death-in-itself, as though it were some Hegelian concept tossed out for the benefit of philosophical seminarians, and the poor speak of it indulgently, happily, even contemptuously, though the contempt is mingled with an appropriate fear.

Octavio Paz, the greatest of modern Mexican poets, has written a study of the Mexican mind, called *The Labyrinth of Solitude*. In this book he pictures the modern Mexican as a man drowning in his own solitude, seeking impatiently for certainties, and finding only one—the certainty that he will die. Instead of being depressed by the discovery, he is jubilant. He will attach himself to this absolute, cling to it, offer himself as a willing victim, seek to approach closer and closer to the mystery, since he is aware of the nothingness and insignificance of life. Death at least promises him an escape from a strange and empty existence, a solitude otherwise without end. His death has a certain grandeur, and it is wholly his own, his ultimate vindication. "Our deaths illuminate our lives." Hence the Mexican's desire to die while performing a grand gesture; he is happiest of all when he is surrounded by his enemies with only one bullet left in the chamber of his revolver. His supreme enjoyment is to die at a moment of passionate elation, laughing in the face of adversity, his enemies at bay.

"The Mexican," writes Octavio Paz, "is familiar with death, jokes about it, caresses it, sleeps with it, celebrates it; it is one of his favorite toys and his most steadfast love." He not only loves death with an abiding and respectful love, but he is also obsessed with it almost to the exclusion of everything else. Every act of his life must relate in some way to his eventual death, and death is the mirror he holds up to life. He boasts about death, his death and all the deaths he will bring about, but he has an uneasy feeling that death is indifferent to all his claims. "We

The water tree at
the National Museum of Anthropology

love the songs and stories in which death laughs and cracks jokes, but all this boastful familiarity does not rid us of the question we all ask: What is death? We have not thought up a new answer. And each time we ask, we shrug our shoulders: Why should I care about death if I have never cared about life?"

The trouble, of course, is that this interpretation leaves so much unexplained. A man cannot spend his days boasting about death; he must earn a living, raise his children, comfort his wife, and see that his mistress acquires some tidbits from his table. He is caught up, like everyone else, in the turbulent flow of life. He is no more solitary than anyone else, and he is far too busy to go hunting after absolutes. If he speaks often about death, it is because the word has become habitual with him, like the habitual swearwords of workmen. The Mexican knows very well that death, far from illuminating his life, merely puts a squalid end to it. So, perhaps, the ever-present skulls are no more than charms or amulets intended to ward off the aggressor, to placate him and lull him into silence or surrender. One suspects that ancestral memory plays its part, for the sugar-candy skulls arranged tier upon tier in the market place look very like the ancient skull racks of Tenochtitlán. The Aztec past is never far away.

On the second of November, the day of the dead, Mexico goes into mourning. On this day the houses are garlanded with marigolds, which have been the *flores de los muertos* since Aztec times. An altar is set up, and offerings are laid on it. Skulls, skeletons, and bones abound, all edible, and a dead man may be invited to feast on his own skull, clearly marked with his name printed in colored sugar. Children wander about, munching skulls. It is like a bone yard, but the bones are very sweet and disappear down living throats. The ceremonies take on the appearance of a small intimate fiesta, gay with flowers, tinsel, and paper garlands. The house has become a small church sacred to *Santísima Muerte*, and it is her litany which is being recited.

There follows the ceremonial journey to the cemetery, everyone wearing his best Sunday clothes. As they walk, someone scatters marigold petals, leaving a trail of flowers. By this trail the dead will know how to make their way back to the house. So they march to the cemetery, burdened with flowers, candles, panniers of food, and many jugs of pulque or tequila, as though they were marching to a feast.

They have come to sprinkle flowers on the grave, to comfort the dead, to sing and lament and get drunk. They will sit there sometimes all night, eating and talking. When night falls, the candles are lit and the whole cemetery is bright in

Mathias Goeritz, a modern designer

the gleam of candles. Every tomb has become a house, with the dead living on the floor below. It is believed that on this day, and this day alone, the dead have been granted the gift of hearing and even of talking. So the dead and the living exchange reminiscences; they plead with one another; and sometimes there are bursts of sudden anger, quarrels, violent colloquies, strange outbursts of laughter. Even in the cemetery there is the air of a fiesta.

Recently the Mexican government has prohibited drinking in the cemeteries. Too many people got drunk, there were too many fights, too many deaths. The cemeteries had become a battlefield; revolvers were whipped out, knives flashed. Today the police march up and down between the tombs on the day of the dead, to preserve the living. But this day is the holy day of *Santísima Muerte*, and she continues to demand sacrifices. The cemetery is her palace, where she feels most abundantly at home and where her laws are always obeyed.

The imaginations of the Mexicans play serenely upon the features of *Santísima Muerte*, but no one ever depicted her better than José Guadalupe Posada, the great engraver who executed some fifteen thousand engravings during the quarter of a century he spent in his small cluttered shop on the Calle de Moneda, just behind the Cathedral. There, in a kind of happy frenzy, sitting over a metal plate with the graver in his hand, in full view of the people passing in the street, his fat face wreathed in smiles, his stomach bulging and pressing against the table, he fought his daily battle with her, for she appeared in nearly all his engravings. He illustrated broadsides, which were printed on pink, green, blue, coral, and yellow paper, and sold for a centavo. Since the broadsides were usually concerned with the inevitable tragedies of the day—murder, suicide, burning buildings, dying children, all the disasters visited on the human race—he had ample opportunity to depict her features. He showed her at her work and in all her moods. Gay, timid, smiling, flushed with victory, sunk in dejection, ferociously ugly, or winsomely charming—he knew exactly how to portray her. He showed her naked, a pure skeleton, or prinked up in her finery. Sometimes he would depict her as an obscene bony insect, half sister to a scorpion, and at other times he would grant her the lineaments of majesty. He could do with skulls what no one else has succeeded in doing—he could make them look alive and infinitely beguiling.

José Guadalupe Posada belongs among the small group of popular engravers who have influenced a whole artistic tradition. As a boy Diego Rivera spent hours

Courtyard, National Museum
of Anthropology

pressing his face against the smudgy windows of the engraver's shop. Clemente Orozco, at the same age, wandered boldly into the shop and reverently collected the slivers of metal that fell from the engraver's plate. There was only one engraving hanging on the walls of the shop. This was Michelangelo's "Last Judgment." Diego Rivera liked to tell the story of how he had once commented that there was no difference between Posada and Michelangelo, for both had the power to give life to the creatures of their imagination. Posada was flattered. "Imagine!" he said. "No one else in the world but you and I knows that it is so." It is not difficult to understand why Posada had so much reverence for Michelangelo's "Last Judgment," for there among the damned *Santísima Muerte* holds her court.

In the most enchanting of all his paintings, "A Dream of a Sunday Afternoon in the Central Alameda Park," Diego Rivera painted all of Mexico strolling through the park on a balmy summer day. There are the flower sellers, the balloon sellers, the sellers of tortillas and sugar candy, and the women in their summer dresses, and all the tyrants and dictators, from Cortés to Don Porfirio Díaz, are pleasantly sunning themselves among the poplars and the ash trees, while the fountains sparkle and a gentle wind curls the feathers of the women's hats. As in a dream the great heroes and villains of the past present themselves. The martyred Francisco Madero doffs his hat. Don Joaquín de la Cantolla waves a Mexican flag as he launches the gaily painted balloon that would carry him to Puebla in 1903; he was the first Mexican balloonist, and therefore deserves an important place. But the most important place is given to *Santísima Muerte*, who appears in all her Sunday morning elegance, smiling her widest smile, wearing an immense hat of spreading ostrich plumes and a stole fashioned out of sheaves of withered corn with a fanged serpent's head protruding at one end and the serpent's rattles protruding from the other, thus demonstrating that she is indeed descended from Coatlícue and wears the appropriate emblems.

She stands in the foreground, gleaming in white bones and white cotton skirts, the center of attraction. Her right hand grasps the hand of a small boy with a pudgy, insolent face, who wears for the occasion a straw hat, his best Sunday suit, and a pair of formidable yellow-and-red stockings. The boy's pockets are stuffed with snakes and toads; he is very pleased with himself; and he is very conscious of his powers. The boy is Diego Rivera, but he is not the only escort of *Santísima Muerte*. Her other escort is José Guadalupe Posada in middle age, with a black mustache, in a derby and with a handkerchief showing at exactly the right angle

Modern painter José Luis Cuevas

178

in the upper pocket of his best Sunday suit. He looks like a man who attends the corner drugstore, portly and amiable, with a fat wife and a brood of robust children. With *Santísima Muerte* as his companion, he has come for his Sunday stroll in Alameda Park with the deliberate intention of enjoying himself. His companion smiles from ear to ear, her bones gleaming, as she rests a delicate hand on his arm, and he offers her his devoted attention by covering her hand with his own to protect and comfort her.

It is a disturbing painting, but an eminently satisfying one. Rivera never painted better, with such brilliant inventiveness and such a lavish display of fresh color. Indeed, the enchanting colors negate the theme of the painting, for a summer morning in the park is by definition the reverse of death. Those gay thronging crowds will not be intimidated by a mere skeleton; they will not follow her; and she is no more than a charade. Take the mask away, and there will be a young woman laughing in the sunlight in all the gaiety of her youth.

There is no real terror in the painting, and we are never completely convinced that death is coming to meet us, or that she ever wore such finery. The setting is absurd, for the immense canvas stands along the wall of the lobby of the Hotel del Prado facing the desk clerks. For years the painting was hidden away because Rivera had insisted on giving one of his heroes a placard inscribed with the words: "God does not exist." There was an uproar; the Catholics were offended, and some students slashed the painting. Toward the end of his life Rivera came to the conclusion that it deserved a better fate, and while he shared the belief inscribed on the placard, he no longer felt any desire to outrage the ninety-six per cent of the Mexican people who were firmly wedded to the Catholic faith. One day in 1956 he climbed a ladder and solemnly painted out the offending placard. Henceforth God was permitted to exist.

As for *Santísima Muerte*, there is some doubt whether she has any real claim to existence. Certainly the Church frowns on her and would be happier if she vanished from the scene. From being Coatlícue she has become a sugar candy, to be gobbled up by children in November, and she inspires no fear, only a kind of brooding affection. The Mexicans know her well, because she is a creature of their imagination, compounded out of memories of Aztec violence and Spanish *morbideza*. In time she will vanish, like all those ancient gods who have outlived their usefulness—or so one says, until one remembers that she is always with us.

Modern sculptor Peter Friedeberg

181

THE THRONES
OF THE GODS

The ancient Aztec gods perished, but something of them remained. They lived on in the imaginations of the Indians and survived in dreams, and sometimes they would emerge from their long silences to assume a Christian disguise. For centuries they had ruled over Mexico, and the ancient traditions did not vanish entirely. The Mexicans are still haunted by them. The conquistadors regarded them as manifestations of the devil in his pride; all were swept away, and in their places they erected images of the Virgin.

In Tenochtitlán the images of the gods were destroyed by fire or hurled into the canals or shattered into a hundred pieces to form the rubble foundations of churches and palaces. But in Mexico City a priest will still occasionally discover the image of an Aztec goddess hidden under the skirts of the Virgin. He will remove the image and smile tolerantly, for such things have been happening for four hundred and fifty years, and it is too late to deplore a custom so deeply ingrained among the people. We learn from Fray Bernardino de Sahagún that as soon as the Franciscan friars arrived in Mexico they would accompany their young Indian pupils to the Aztec temples and order them to destroy the temples completely, brick by brick, until not a vestige remained, until it was impossible to tell that there had ever been a temple in that place. The earth was leveled and raked over, everything that could conceivably refer to the cult of the god was destroyed, and on the place where the temple had been they erected a church. Fray Bernardino de Sahagún knew better than anyone that the ancient Aztec gods remained.

He knew because it was his purpose to know, because he spent a great part of his life enthusiastically studying them for his great work *General History of the Things of New Spain,* which was lost for centuries and not published until two hundred and fifty years after his death. His superiors disapproved of the work. They noted that he showed a great sympathy for the Aztec civilization and he seemed to have a special fondness for the Aztec gods. Accordingly, with the excuse

Paper stand in front
of the Sagrario Metropolitano

that there was not sufficient paper to print the work, they delayed its publication indefinitely. The manuscript was divided up among the different religious houses in Mexico, and they hoped that nothing more would be heard of it. Finally it was discovered in a remote convent in northern Spain, and published for the first time in Mexico City in 1829. A year later it appeared in the magnificent royal folios called *The Antiquities of Mexico,* published by Lord Kingsborough, who died in a debtors' prison in Dublin, having failed to pay the paper manufacturer for the immense quantities of paper needed in those books produced without any regard for cost. Fray Bernardino would have been pleased. At long last the work to which he had dedicated his life appeared in two sumptuous editions.

Fray Bernardino accomplished what no one else accomplished. While memories were still fresh, he wrote down the legends of the Aztecs, described their customs, transcribed their songs, related their history. He had a great affection for the Indians, and this affection spilled over until it embraced their entire way of life. He arrived in Mexico in 1529 when the memory of the Conquest was still fresh and Cortés was still Captain General of New Spain, and he lived through the reigns of the early viceroys. From the lips of men who had known Moctezuma he heard the Aztec account of the Conquest, which differed in important particulars from the Spanish account. Speaking the Náhuatl language, living for long periods in villages which no other Spaniards ever entered, he became the champion of the Aztecs, to the disgust of his superiors, who complained that he knew too much about the Aztecs and too little about missionary work.

He was a slight man with deep-set melancholy eyes and an appearance of studied simplicity, but this was merely a mask for an extraordinarily rich and complex mind. He had the modern temper. He was not content to write down the legends as they were related to him, but he was continually checking his sources. He would consult one authority, then another, then a third. He would, for example, ask an old Aztec priest to make a drawing of Quetzalcóatl and describe his robes, his headdress, his regalia, what he was wearing on his feet, and what he was carrying in his hands, and he would write it all down at the priest's dictation. Then from another priest in another village many miles away he would receive another drawing of Quetzalcóatl, and he would continue to consult the priests and elders of other villages until he was assured that he had achieved a final and accurate portrait of the god, his legends, and his powers. The Indian gods were very strange

Students at an 18th-century fountain

indeed, for they went through many manifestations and wore many disguises. Fray Bernardino describes them convincingly and sympathetically. With their rainbow-colored plumes, their smoking mirrors and flowering bones, they emerge as figures of dazzling beauty and formidable power.

At Teotihuacán, not far from Mexico City, we can almost glimpse the presence of the gods in their splendor. In that ancient city stretching over six square miles, once the center of an empire, two pyramids arise of such awesome proportions that at first the mind refuses to accept their reality. The Pyramid of the Sun is two hundred and ten feet high and covers fifty-five thousand square yards; it has been calculated that it weighs three million tons. The Pyramid of the Moon is one hundred and thirty-eight feet high, but its proportions are such that it seems not to lie in the shadow of the greater pyramid but to support it. These pyramids were built long before the Aztecs entered the Valley of Mexico. It is not surprising that the Aztecs attributed them to the giants who once inhabited the earth, a belief strengthened by the discovery of fossil bones of elephants, which they thought to be human bones, in the neighborhood. But it is not only the size of the pyramids that inspires a feeling of awe. The Pyramid of the Moon stands at the end of a long avenue known since Aztec times as the Road of the Dead. The Pyramid of the Sun lies to the east of this road some five hundred and fifty yards to the south. Between these two pyramids an astonishing architectural tension has been created. They exist for one another, belong to one another, being deliberately built in such a way that they reinforce and echo one another, and this is brought about by their careful placing in the landscape with the hills rising behind them, and because the Pyramid of the Moon, being on higher ground, stands at exactly the same height as the Pyramid of the Sun. While the pyramids at Giza are scattered over the desert in confusion, the two pyramids at Teotihuacán exist in a close and living relationship to one another.

Teotihuacán means "the place where men become gods." Fray Bernardino de Sahagún asked the Indians what was meant by the name and received the reply in the form of a song:

> They called this place Teotihuacán
> because the kings were buried here,
> for the ancients said:

Benito Juárez memorial monument,
Avenida Juárez

186

"When we die, truly we become gods,
we awaken out of the dream
and begin to live again,
for this is our happiness."
And so they spoke to the dead, saying:
"Lord or lady, arise,
already the dawn is red,
already the sun is rising,
and the flame-colored birds are singing,
and the many-colored butterflies are flying."
And so when anyone dies,
they say he has become a god,
and to say: "He has become a god"
means: "He is dead."

According to the song, Teotihuacán was the burial place of kings and noblemen, but no graves have been found near the two immense pyramids. When Fray Bernardino was writing, sixteen hundred years had passed since the building of the pyramids, and for five hundred years no one had lived in the city which spread out on both sides of the great processional avenue. It is possible that the Aztecs had already forgotten who built the pyramids, and they would visit these temples as one might go to some old and very venerable shrines which were revered simply for their antiquity.

To this day no one knows who built the pyramids. By A.D. 600 the civilization of Teotihuacán was already declining, and by A.D. 900 the entire city appears to have been abandoned. It was a very large city, with a population of perhaps a quarter of a million people, but it left no written history, no songs or legends by which it might be remembered. Fire, famine, disease, invasion, erosion, earthquakes, social decay, intellectual and aesthetic exhaustion, a curse laid on the city—all those catastrophes that are commonly put forward to explain the extinction of empires—fail to carry conviction. We do not know what happened, and we cannot guess. For hundreds of years painters, sculptors, and architects erect monuments of extraordinary grandeur and authority; suddenly it is all over. Nothing remains except the pyramids, the small palaces, many of them still unexcavated, and the great courtyard, a mile down the road, with its small temple dedicated to Quetzal-cóatl and Tlaloc.

In its relationship to the two great pyramids this small temple is so perfectly placed that it appears to have been designed for no other purpose than to balance them. Set in the middle of a vast courtyard, it gives an effect of height and spaciousness from its very isolation, its lonely grandeur. Where the great pyramids shout, this temple merely whispers. The mathematicians have calculated the exact spot where this temple should be in order to produce the purest enchantment. They have solved the problems of space with breath-taking ease.

In all Indian architecture there is the attempt to create vibrant and vivid space. At Palenque and in the great plaza at Tenochtitlán, and here again at Teotihuacán, we see them creating a complex architecture of space. The temples balance one another and exist in harmony with one another; and the space between and around them has its own harmony. The space between them was so calculated that each temple had its appropriate air to breathe in, and at the same time the temples reflected, honored, and reinforced one another. The Aztecs were designing communities of temples, and thought in communal terms. They were not celebrating the individual gods, but the community of gods. With delicacy and restraint, with mathematical precision, and with a profound feeling for the gods, they fashioned these superb monuments.

As we see them now, bare of all their former ornament, the pyramids of Teotihuacán appear as vast geometric designs. Almost they are abstractions of power, and therefore they are very satisfying to the modern taste. But from painted pottery shards found nearby we know that these temples were brilliantly colored, with fantastic ornamentation. Once there was painted stucco in all the colors of the rainbow, with crowns of feathers, fishtails, circles, crescent moons, frets, steps, and jagged bands like Chinese cloud bands. The pyramids of the Sun and Moon were a blaze of color from top to bottom. So, too, was the original temple to Quetzalcóatl and Tlaloc, which was built over a much older and more decorative one. The old temple was revealed by archaeologists who sliced through the adobe brickwork to reveal the hidden core, which is heavily ornamented with the two enormous eyes of Tlaloc and the serpent head of Quetzalcóatl in his plumes. Because there is a very narrow catwalk to bring you only a few inches away from these gods, the effect is of being propelled violently into their embrace. Traces of color were found, and

Tepotzotlán Convent, Tepotzotlán

archaeologists from the Museum of Anthropology were able to reconstruct part of the façade in its original colors. The head of the plumed serpent was purple, but he wore a surprisingly delicate collar of yellow petals. Like Tlaloc, he was a god who brought blessings to men, and no human sacrifices were offered to him. Nor, except on very rare occasions, were human sacrifices offered to Tlaloc, whom we see again in a painting found in one of the nearby palaces in all the majesty of his green robes, while green plumes sprout from his head and green tusks sprout from his mouth. He was not in the least malevolent; on the contrary, he was one of the gods who bring abundant life to the earth.

In Teotihuacán a great civilization perished, but it did not wholly perish. The influence of Teotihuacán culture was far-reaching, extending over the Valley of Mexico, and over Oaxaca in the south, and Mayan Yucatan in the southeast. Nearly seven hundred miles to the southeast, in the highlands of Guatemala, there are tombs and temples which are so clearly derived from Teotihuacán that it has been supposed that conquerors brought the culture with them. The marks of this culture are readily discerned in the shapes given to the gods, and in a certain austerity and tendency to abstraction and in the great elegance of the temples. The pyramids of Teotihuacán are to be counted among the great achievements of mankind, and it is not surprising that a civilization charged with so much energy should leave its stamp over so many distant regions.

In Cholula, half a day's easy drive from Mexico City, on the road to Vera Cruz, there is an even larger pyramid, though it is less imposing because its shape has not yet been revealed. One sees a green mountain, and it is almost beyond belief that this mountain has been built with human hands. Fray Bernardino de Sahagún, who visited it, wrote very sensibly that while all the evidence granted to the eyes suggested that it was made by God, many had entered into its tunnels and found it made of brick. This incredibly massive pyramid covers twenty-five acres, and stands one hundred and eight feet high.

Today the archaeologists are at work, cutting away at the lower stages, revealing platforms and galleries and intricately designed floors of colored stone. Tunnels leading into the interior have been reopened, and you can see the exact point where one pyramid begins and another ends, for this pyramid, too, has been formed out of many superimposed pyramids. In these dark depths you occasionally come upon the strange red dragon-insects, which derive from Teotihuacán, painted

Interior of a church
by architect Juan Sordo Madaleno

193

on the walls. The guide's lamp flickers; the dragon waves his antenna, blood-red, trembling in the silver light; and then the lamp goes out, and you are somewhere near the center of the largest pyramid of the world in a darkness without end.

This temple was dedicated to Quetzalcóatl, and it was already in ruins when Cortés passed through Cholula on his way to Tenochtitlán. He knew he was being identified with Quetzalcóatl, but he appears to have shown very little interest in the god. He made some casual inquiries and learned that Quetzalcóatl was the god of the air and the reputed founder of the city, "and they say he was a virgin of the utmost austerity, and dressed in white cotton, and kept certain green stones as though they were relics, including a stone carved in the shape of a monkey's head." He knew that Cholula was the holy city of the Indians and he had counted the steps leading up to the top of the temple—there were one hundred and twenty.

Like Apollo, Quetzalcóatl was the god of light and air, and of the human intelligence. He was the earth-bound creature who learned to fly, the serpent who swept across the skies. Like Apollo, too, he had his destructive aspect, for the Aztecs identified him with Huitzilopochtli, the god of the sun and of war. Quetzalcóatl was the god of youth and human energy, all that was dazzling and beautiful and therefore touched with immortality. He had risen from his own funeral pyre to become the evening and morning stars. It was said of him that he was wise above all the generations of men, and had once, as a king, ruled so justly that he was ever afterward regarded as a model of kingship. Fray Bernardino de Sahagún inquired deeply into his origins and uncovered texts suggesting that in the beginning he was no more than the servant of Tlaloc, being "one of those who sweep the paths for the rain gods, so that they might bring rain." But soon he rose to the level of the master and became the dominant power among the gods. An Aztec song has been preserved which depicts Quetzalcóatl in his glory:

> I am the only flower, the new, the glorious one.
> Born from water I am, born a youth already and a man.
> I came forth from the blue homes of fishes, a new and most glorious
>   god.
> I shine like the sun; my mother dwelt in the mansions of the dawn,
> She who was fiery-colored as the quechol bird, a new and most
>   glorious flower.

Right
University of Mexico Library,
with mural by Juan O'Gorman

Next two pages
Plaza of the Three Cultures

So I came forth to the earth, even to the market place, like a man:
I am Quetzalcóatl, the great and glorious god.
Be tender then under the flower bush as fiery-colored as the quechol,
Listen to the quechol singing to the gods,
Listen to the quechol singing alone on the river-bank.
Hear him piping along the river in the house of reeds.
Would that my flowers ceased from dying!
Our flesh is as flowers, even as the flowers in the place of flowers.
O she goes to the market place, bearing Xochiquetzal to the market,
She speaks at Cholula and startles my heart.
My heart is startled by her, nor is there an end to it.
The priests know her:
Where the merchants sell green jade ear-rings she is known.
In the place of wonders she is there.
Sleep, sleep, sleep. I fold my hands in sleep.
O woman, I sleep.

This mysterious poem was sung by fasters at the festival of Quetzalcóatl. They are singing about a god of great gentleness and brightness, associated with many legends deriving from many sources, rich in beauty and ambiguity. In him there seemed to be concentrated all the nobility of the Indian people who created him. Sometimes even now, as you gaze at the giant pyramids at Teotihuacán and Cholula, you find yourself wondering whether the Aztec gods will one day return to their thrones.

Modern office buildings
on the Paseo de la Reforma

THE SPLENDORS
OF THE CITY

In the blue light of early morning or the bright sunflower yellow of early afternoon, Mexico City assumes the dimensions of a dream where everything is a little larger, brighter, and more desirable than in other cities. The fountains flash with a dazzling whiteness, the flower sellers arrange their flowers as though determined to create explosions of violent color, and the glass buildings shimmer and dance and reel against the perfect skies. The intensity of color has a hallucinatory quality; the skies have been washed clear and everything looks new, as though it had been painted that very morning. Among those rockets and Catherine wheels of exploding colors, the fountains and the flowers, there is the effect of descending deep into an enchanted sea, finding at the seabed, among the trees of coral and the bones of long-extinct fish, a world brighter and more crystalline than any that exists on the sea's surface.

In Mexico, and especially in Mexico City, color is palpable. A certain voluminous rust red, a peculiarly vivid vitreous green, and a yellow that flares like a kerosene flame are especially remarkable. You see these colors on the serapes of the Indians, sometimes dramatically interposed with bars of violet, black, or white, and you see the same colors in the painted pottery and sculpture of the Aztecs. The cups from which Moctezuma drank were made from the lustrous black and rust-red Cholula ware, and long before Moctezuma the great temple to Quetzal-cóatl at Teotihuacán was painted in those same reds, yellows, and greens. Indeed, all the Indian temples were painted in those stark, earthy colors, and you see them again in the codices, those histories written in pictures by a people who preferred to paint faces and emblems rather than to submit themselves to the tyranny of an alphabet. You can say very nearly all you want to say in pictures, and these painted codices have a full, lusty life of their own such as you will never find on the printed page.

Red, yellow, and green—but what reds, what yellows, what greens! In that

rarefied air the sweetness of those colors can be tasted on the mouth; color has become a way of life, the purest of satisfactions. It is because color is so much a part of life, so necessary to the Mexicans, that artists took possession of the walls of schools, churches, and government offices in order to transform them into a delirium of color, scarcely caring what or how they painted so long as they could hang their rainbows. At the entrance to the Museum of the Cultures, formerly the mint, in the Calle de Moneda, you find Tomayo's portrait of a Spanish Republican soldier heroically clubbing the Fascists. In Chapultepec Castle Orozco has painted a gigantic portrait of Juárez in the colors of the flaming sunset, while below him an elongated Maximilian, wrapped in his cerements, the features modeled on the terrible death mask, with a rippling, silken, yellow beard added as an afterthought, is borne on the shoulders of his French generals to the waiting ships; but Maximilian is no more than subliminal decoration, and the eye sees only the blaze of the red-hot sunset. On the walls of the National Palace Diego Rivera has painted his distorted version of Mexican history dominated by a monstrous spindle-shanked Cortés at one end and a heavily bearded Marx at the other end. They are poster paintings, very nearly intolerable as works of art, but the gaiety of the coloring and the brilliance of the flat design make them endurable. If the paintings had been hung upside down they would have been just as effective. What is needed— what the Mexican is determined to have—is splashes of ripe color all around him. Though the paintings belong to their time, being so dated that they are sometimes scarcely comprehensible, their colors belong to all time. In Mexico everyone is a painter or looks at the world through a painter's eyes.

Not, of course, that Mexico City is everywhere full of color. There are places where the colors have been burned away by poverty and despair. The slum colonies, known as *vecindados*, cluster in the shadows of palaces; they are windowless cells, where disease breeds unchecked and the poor congregate in helpless fury, living four or five in a dark room no larger than the inside of a truck. In these rooms the poor have developed a fierce defensive culture of their own; they conspire against the rest of the world, using knives and revolvers as their chosen weapons. In the long run they are less dangerous than the Mexican bureaucrats who have inherited all the intellectual diseases of Spanish bureaucracy and have, in addition, acquired some characteristic diseases of their own. Of the seven deadly vices they are most addicted to pride and *acedia*. Wherever the Mexican bureaucrat goes, he leaves a

Modern Mexico—apartment house

permanent clot of darkness; and though his chief aim is to reduce the poor to a state of unendurable frustration, he is not averse to inflicting the same punishment on the rich. Government offices appear to be rooted in the nineteenth century; the post office, the tourist office, and the various offices for the protection and betterment of the Indians are afflicted with a dark and brooding melancholia that effectively prevents them from doing their work efficiently. Letters rarely arrive on time; the tourist office is perfectly capable of giving the wrong information; and the Indians are left to their own resources. The revolutions were abortive, for they left the bureaucrats in full possession of their powers.

The young architects of the present day have cut through the bureaucratic red tape. With magnificent effrontery they have built skyscrapers in all the colors of the rainbow. Remembering Tenochtitlán, they were determined to erect great painted towers, using the steel and glass of the present age. Unlike New York architects, they use steel and glass imaginatively, and they are not bound by the unwritten law stating that architecture consists in designing boxes. The Mexican architects shape their buildings to conform to the landscape. One of the most successful and beautiful buildings is a skyscraper shaped like a slender triangle with walls of golden glass. During the thirties they deliberately designed buildings with scarcely any window space, so that the outside walls could be covered with shimmering fields of mosaics. The best of these is the University Library, with its spinning wheels and sunbursts set amid the legends of the Aztecs and the symbols of the Conquest, a huge square building on stilts that somehow suggests lightness and grace. The University itself is a riot of color, with vast murals stretching across the walls, while the glinting mosaics of the Library tower over them all. The Public Works building, with mosaics by Rivera and O'Gorman, has not fared so well, perhaps because it lacked an essential simplicity. No single theme runs through the mosaics that crowd its colored walls; smog and the yellow dust from the lake bed have muted the colors and have given a somber, prisonlike appearance to the building.

In Tlatelolco, in what used to be the northern suburbs of the city, now very close to the center, the architects have had a field day. Near the ruins of an Aztec temple and in full view of an Aztec ball court, facing the old Church of Santiago and the College of Santa Cruz, they built a complex of yellow, red, and orange apartment houses, a school, and the marble Ministry of Foreign Affairs. The effect

Insurance company building,
Paseo de la Reforma

is magical, for the apartment houses have exactly the right coloring to display the church and the ruins to their best advantage. There is a sense of spaciousness, of the air flowing freely among the buildings, which represent the three cultures of Mexico. The church is superb. Through the high windows a purple light pours over the bare walls on which, here and there, we can see the faint outlines of ancient wall paintings. All the baroque ornaments that once adorned the church have been removed, and on the altar there is a single gold screen showing Santiago, who is St. James, the warrior saint, on horseback. The Saint looks suspiciously like Cortés, who received the surrender of the eighteen-year-old Cuauhtémoc, the last Emperor of the Aztecs, near this spot. As you come out of the church you find an inscription, reading:

> On the 13th of August, 1521, Tlatelolco, heroically defended by Cuauhtémoc, fell to the power of Hernán Cortés.
> This was neither a triumph nor a defeat, but the painful birth of the mestizo people who form the Mexico of today.

The words are carved on a large marble plaque, and are heavy with meaning, with doubt, with ambiguity, and with hesitations, for the statement affirms what cannot be affirmed. It implies that the young Emperor had defended Tlatelolco to the last. In fact, he was fleeing from the city in a boat when he was captured by the Spaniards and brought shivering and trembling to the feet of Cortés. *Ne fué trionfo ni derrota.* . . . But the triumph of Cortés was such that all Mexican history would henceforth bear the imprint of his mind, and the defeat was overwhelming. Here, or very close to this spot, Cortés took possession of his vast Mexican empire; his triumph was also a defeat, and here the new Mexico had its painful birth.

The Plaza of the Three Cultures shows the three cultures standing peacefully together. The brilliantly colored apartment houses look down on the church in which Juan Diego, the Indian who spoke with the Virgin at Tepeyac, was baptized and on the College of Santa Cruz, where Fray Bernardino de Sahagún learned from the Indians the history of the Aztec empire. And the church looks down on the ball park and the broken walls of the pyramid that Moctezuma once climbed hand in hand with Cortés. Like the Zócalo, the Plaza of the Three Cultures is one of those rare places where history accumulated; and as you walk across the green ball park or climb the pyramids or enter the quiet church, you are very close to the heart of the mystery.

Office building on the Paseo de la Reforma

Here, in the evening, beside the poplars and a small lake, in the silence that descends like drumbeats over all the plazas of Mexico at the time of vespers, the world seems to come to a sudden stop. In the hour that is neither night nor day, the sunlight on the painted windows flares, the church becomes incandescent, the ball park sinks away, and the reddish stones of the pyramids catch the sunset. It is at that moment, in the sudden hush of evening, when the colors change, becoming more intense and more alive, glowing like coals, that the plaza comes into its own, affirming quietly and insistently, in the words of the Aztec chronicler, that "as long as the world may endure, the fame and glory of this city will never perish."

INDEX

211